THE
NEW SHAPE
OF
MINISTRY

THE
NEW SHAPE
OF
MINISTRY

TAKING ACCOUNTABILITY SERIOUSLY

ROBERT G. KEMPER

Abingdon   Nashville

THE NEW SHAPE OF MINISTRY

Copyright © 1979 by Abingdon

Library of Congress Cataloging in Publication Data

KEMPER, ROBERT G
  The new shape of ministry.
  1. Clergy—Office. I. Title.
  BV660.2.K47   253   78-12256

ISBN 0-687-27874-0

MANUFACTURED BY THE PARTHENON PRESS AT
NASHVILLE, TENNESSEE, UNITED STATES OF AMERICA

In Appreciation

This book is dedicated to
three very special, very different women:

for Margie who helps me live
for Eleanor who helps me see
for Joan who helps me write

An Invitation

You are invited to participate in the preliminary planning for a convocation on the parish ministry, now meeting in the pages of this book. The purpose of this meeting is to stimulate your thoughts about the ministerial profession. You are being invited to participate because you care about the profession (or you would not have entered its practice) and because you—and only you—can alter its shape.

This book contains an agenda for parish clergy. By its very nature any agenda is manipulative. An agenda defines the parameters of discussion and action and directs participants' energies and attention to certain specific areas. Many attempts have been made in print and in face-to-face consultations to analyze and alter the ministerial profession.

The agenda for this convocation is different. First, no face-to-face meeting will be scheduled until you demand one. This book offers only preliminary papers to such an eventuality. Second, these papers do not solicit your affirmation of their particular form. Rather, what is solicited is your affirmation that this agenda is the right one for the ministerial profession at this particular time. In short, your acceptance of this invitation is not under the condition that you agree with all its provisions, but that you concur that the issues facing the profession have been rightly named in these pages.

Please read the agenda on the following pages. Read it first for verification. Do the specifics of this agenda relate to your personal experience in the practice of ministry or to the experiences of your colleagues in the profession? At this first reading, categories are more important than substance. Substance will be developed in subsequent chapters, and at that time correction and dissent will be encouraged. But during this introductory look, seek to verify whether the realities confronting the ministerial system have been identified. What these realities mean and what can be done about them could become the substance of a convocation for parish clergy. For now, let us search for the issues facing our profession.

An Agenda
For the Parish Clergy

An analysis of the factors that currently shape the ministerial profession. Who says what a parish minister is and does? Who says what practitioners need in preparatory and continuing education? Who determines conditions and location of work? Who sets the pace, style, and patterns in the profession? These questions may surprise you, but your answer to them forms a necessary prelude to the subsequent advocacies.

BE IT RESOLVED: That practitioners of the minsterial

profession become responsible for the orientation of beginning parish clergy.

This analyst deplores the nature of the first pastorate experience. Present practitioners must know that there is a better way to begin the pattern of collegial ministry.

AGENDA ITEM 2: DEFINING SUCCESS   53

BE IT RESOLVED: That parish clergy define success for themselves.

This analysis shows that avoiding the subject leads practitioners to extraneous and spurious definitions of success. Such definitions will not disappear if clergy ignore the subject. This advocacy calls for present practitioners to seize the initiative and begin to define for themselves what constitutes advancement, growth, and accomplishment in the profession.

AGENDA ITEM 3: CONTINUING EDUCATION 63

BE IT RESOLVED: That parish clergy seize the initiative in procuring the education they need for growth.

The analyst criticizes the mediocrity and stagnation of the profession. Clergy have become consumers of educational offerings. This advocacy calls for a new aggressiveness on the part of clergy to seek the continuing education that they desire for their own personal growth.

AGENDA ITEM 4: SALARIES   71

BE IT RESOLVED: That parish clergy receive higher salaries.

The analysis moves beyond the obvious, and beyond the baser motives for higher salaries. It exposes a deeper, darker factor in the low salaries of clergy. This advocacy offers alternative first steps toward greater fiscal maturity.

AGENDA ITEM 5: PLACEMENT   83

BE IT RESOLVED: That there be greater peer participation in the placement system.

The analyst notes grumblings about placement in differing church polities and concludes that the problem is not one of polity, but of changing expectations which overload the placement machinery. More is involved than finding the right person for the right position. The advocacy suggests that with so much at stake in placement, more diffusion of authority would be preferred, especially among those directly affected by the authority.

AGENDA ITEM 6: USE OF TIME   95

BE IT RESOLVED: That parish clergy work less and play more.

Analysis suggests that clergy are workaholics, to the detriment of their families and maybe even to the church. A sinister suspicion is advanced: clergy may be lacking in faith. This advocacy calls for clergy to control their time and take time for themselves.

AGENDA ITEM 7: SELECTIVITY FOR OLDER MINISTERS   105

BE IT RESOLVED: That retirement be a time of maximum freedom for retired ministers.

The analyst laments the scandal regarding retired clergy: they are ignored by present practitioners. The pain of retired clergy is caused not only by loss of status, but also by curtailment of freedom in their lives. The advocacy points to ways of involving retired clergy and of increasing their freedom. A surprising bonus of this advocacy is a solution to the "clergy surplus" problem.

A WORKSHOP ON PROFESSIONAL ASSOCIATIONS   117

- The means of change
- The shape and style of a professional association of clergy
- The function of a professional association of clergy
- A report from the field

ADJOURNMENT AND BENEDICTION   131

Background Notes

Let the following pages serve as background notes on how and why this agenda was formulated. I hope your own experience verifies this agenda as worthy of consideration. But I do owe you a wider explanation of the assumptions, history, and purpose of these ideas.

First, some personal introductions are in order. The contents of this book are more experiential than intellectual. I have been an ordained minister for eighteen years. My personal stewardship of ordination has had two forms: I have been and am now a practicing parish minister; I also had a five-year tenure as founding editor of *The Christian*

Ministry, an ecumenical, professional journal for clergy. Both vocational experiences are relevant to this book. As a parish minister I have experienced these issues; as a magazine editor I have conceptualized them and shared them in personal addresses to multiple groups of clergy—of all denominations, from coast to coast. This is the first time these conceptions have been put to print, but it is not the first time they have been advanced before my colleagues. Therefore, I know some of the objections and critiques they are likely to evoke. More about that later; for now let me continue to trace the origins of this agenda.

I must identify myself as one who has been well served by the church system. (I hope that affirmation is reciprocal.) I want you to know that I am not a malcontent; I have no hidden agenda, no axe to grind against anyone, or any system. I call no one to revolution because of intolerable conditions. Quite the contrary, I bother to write these words because of my affection for the church and its clergy. St. Paul prefaced his famous love chapter in the Letter to the Corinthians, saying, "I will show you a still more excellent way." In that same spirit, I offer these criticisms and complaints about things as they are because I have a dream of things as they might yet be. The publication of this book may be nothing more than one man holding a banner aloft to see if a parade will form behind that standard. Despite the open invitation on the first page, I have no illusions that all clergy of all churches would want to be together to discuss their common (and uncommon) profession.

Further, my professional experience, like yours, is very particular and cannot be universalized to embrace clergy of all sorts and conditions of clergy. The accidents of my life alone prevent this: I am white, middle-aged, and male. These accidents may be categorical majorities in the profession, but in our day "normalcy" is being challenged, and one must remember the narrow focus of one's own experience and welcome the contributions of other persons of different accidents of life. But in identifying the particularities of my experience I must single out one which has shaped my conception of the agenda before us. My pastoral ministry has been in free church polity; therefore, congregational government with its attendant freedoms and limitations is the one I know best. No doubt my narrow experience was broadened by work on the ecumenical journal, but the fact remains: I have never been appointed by a district superintendent, tried to change a presbytery, or confronted a bishop. This is not an apology for my free church experience, but an explanation of the form of this book.

In presenting this material orally with clergy of differing traditions, I first tried to adapt it as I perceived the necessities among the connectional churches. This, I soon learned, was disastrous. It disclosed the paucity of my conceptions about Christendom. But in the midst of those well-meaning disasters I made an important discovery: that I need not attempt to adapt these advocacies to ecclesiastical polities; clergy themselves will make these adaptations. With the assurance that these general propositions can be adapted to a particular polity, I was encouraged to express them in this individual form. I believe these advocacies can be reconstituted because they are transcendent. Sometimes, hurt and embittered clergy think a change of denomination will resolve their conflicts. Usually, they are wrong; most of the time all they really change are the set of problems. The discovery of transcendence and adaptation makes it possible to write for a whole profession, irrespective of differing polities.

A similar disclaimer needs to be made about the lack of a theology, or more correctly, about the implicit theology, that is here contained. It is impudent and foolish to write a book on the ministry without beginning with a doctrine of the church, or of Christ's authority, or of God's design for the world and the church in that world. There is not enough surgical gauze on the earth to bind the wounds I am destined to receive from theologians who review this book! This may not stay my theological critics, but one of them, John MacQuarrie, offers an insight that helps to express my argument. Writing in *Principles of Christian Theology,* he observes that the church is both a theological and a sociological entity, and we err if we subordinate or elevate one at the expense of the other. I would *like* to say that this book is about the sociology of the church and its ministry, not the theology. But that violates MacQuarrie's basic insight and invites the criticism of sociologists of religion and religious institutions. The point I do want to make is that this book is neither a theological fish nor a sociological fowl. It is based on pastoral instinct and intuition. Now, we are back to my experience and yours. Nothing would please me more than for this book to stimulate a rigorous theological and sociological inquiry to authenticate or refute my pastoral instincts and intuitions. Until that happens I leave you with a book that may be shallow in theology and sociology, but that invites you to bring to your reading such data and faith as seem relevant.

In the labor of writing these pages I asked myself, Why am I doing this? My time and my hands are full with the practice of ministry. I did not need an interlude from other matters. What motivates me is simple to state, but complex to apply: I care. I care about the church. I care about the ministerial profession. I care about particular persons who struggle and triumph in little and great ways in their practice. I even care about those in the profession that I never expect to know, but who have my admiration when they function well and my disappointment when they do not.

The way I have shaped the agenda makes this book seem shamelessly chauvinistic about the clergy. Aren't lay people in the church? Why not write an agenda of the laity? Maybe I will—some day. But this is not a book about everything, it is only about a small part of the whole church: the clergy. My advocacies for the clergy are neither chauvinistic nor against lay people. I believe the whole enterprise of the church will be strengthened when both partners have a sense of who they are, what they can and should do—or cannot and should not do. In conceptualizing the problems of the clergy I have never believed that what ails us is them. What ails us is us. This book attempts to work with us—the clergy.

It contains several other implicit assumptions. First, that there is a church system or systems within churchly institutions. Professor MacQuarrie has warned us that we ignore them at our own peril. Systems are not inexorable, immutable processes, rather, they are composite components functioning together to produce a result. The Christian community has many components, one being clergy, and what we do as clergy cannot but have an effect.

Thus follows the second assumption, the power of intentionality in ministry. The church does not have to function as it does just because it has always functioned that way. It has enormous elasticity and can accommodate many conflicting claims and affirmations. My task in this book is not to change the church, but to help clergy be more conscious of the ways they perpetuate—or could alter—the systems that affect the ministerial profession. I said earlier that I am not a malcontent within the church. I am not because I have seen and experienced the ways in which clergy can change and grow in the church and how the church profits and grows as a result of these changes. By becoming more intentional about their profession, clergy can strengthen the whole church. That is caring for the church and its ministry at the highest level.

A word about the methodology of caring, another major assumption in this book. My third assumption is that there is enormous power in groups. Many of us have known personal growth through our relationships with lay groups in our churches. But we have not realized the power we could have in peer relationships. Not power to gang up on the laity, or the system, but power to affect the church system by liberating and enriching ourselves as practitioners. Traditionally, clergy do not have strong peer associations because of who they are. Writing in *Minister on the Spot,* Yale's James Dittes categorizes clergy as mediating types. Most of the time we tend to function as brokers and negotiators between conflicting groups. The price of having that characteristic (if you want to look at it that way) is that clergy tend to be less likely to have strong peer relationships.

If that is correct, will we be able to develop strong peer relationships? That question, brothers and sisters, is what this book comes to test. And it is shaped around an agenda because my hunch is that clergy do not have an inclination toward peer relationships, but we can rally around common issues. Hence my series of advocacies transcend theological questions, polity questions, and sociopsychological tendencies, in an attempt to build a coalition of clergy around common issues that can change the church system and enable clergy and laity to meet as adults for mutual growth. Can this be done? I do not know, but I care enough to write these words and see what results.

Finally, I will admit to one form of chauvinism. This book is aimed at parish clergy, and I refer to the practice of parish ministry as a profession. In so doing I may incur the wrath of two groups I do not wish to alienate: ministers who are not parish clergy, and parish clergy who dislike using the word "profession" to describe their calling. Hoping to keep the attention of both groups, I offer the rationale used by James Glasse in *Profession: Minister.* He asserts that a characteristic of professional work is that it is done within an institution—doctors in hospitals, lawyers in courts, teachers in schools, etc. Clergy who work within the institutional church—bureaucracy, chaplaincy, mission—are also practicing professionals. And, like parish clergy of differing polities, you quasi-parish clergy will have to interpolate these advocacies within your particular frame of reference. I trust that you will.

I hope these background notes about the assumptions and purpose of these ideas have informed and not distracted you from the unfolding agenda. If the keynote, advocacies, and plan for a clergy organization move you to action, please do not tell me about it. Begin talking with your colleagues about your way of caring for the ministerial profession.

Robert G. Kemper
First Congregational Church
Western Springs, Illinois
Spring, 1978

Keynote:
Who is Responsible
for the Parish Clergy?

Posing the Question

These analytical questions form the basis of the subsequent advocacies. My purpose is to identify factors and forces that influence and shape the ministerial profession. Obviously, the factors discussed here are not an exhaustive list. Conspicuously absent are factors of faith and theology, sociology and psychology, history and location—mighty factors in the conduct of ministry. But I contend that their absence does not invalidate this analysis. Under scrutiny here is not how faith is applied to the ministerial vocation, but how people of faith perform their functions within an institutional framework and the factors that affect their performance.

Furthermore, this analysis is highly selective. The factors I have chosen are those amenable to change: customs or procedures, even common understandings, that have long functioned within the church. These factors are often assumed to be "givens" because they come with the territory. Yet they are not immutable laws of God and man. When anthropologists study a foreign culture, the first 15 minutes of their observations are critical. This time frame may not be accurate, but the principle is: the longer one lives within a particular culture, the less one notices its differentiations and the more one adapts to its customs. Such is the case with ministerial practitioners. Experience within the profession may simply mean that one has adapted oneself to the accepted patterns within the church system. So my criterion for selecting factors that affect the ministry is intentionally aimed at stimulating your inquiry and prompting a dialogue in response. What are the factors affecting the conduct of ministry that can be altered for the betterment of the profession? Must these factors affect the parish clergy the way they do?

The focus of this analysis is expressed in the keynote: Who is *responsible* for the parish clergy? Several answers come quickly to mind, which I reject with equal speed—*I* am responsible for the parish clergy—wrong. Clergy is a plural noun, I am singular. The collaborative or collegial factor is missing. Another quick response is to say that the church is responsible for the parish clergy. This reply is held widely among clergy, but its popularity is the result of misreading the question. In naming the different gifts of the Spirit to the Corinthians, St. Paul never says that the church is directly responsible for each of those gifts. And that's my point. Within the Christian community there are systems or orders. These systems do interact, and they feed each other, but there is not necessarily an umbilical cord that functions like a lifeline from one part to the other. Simply put, clergy function within the church; pietistically put, they have consecrated their lives to Christ and the church. But that does not mean that the church is responsible for the clergy.

In this analysis the factors affecting the clergy can be explored by sharpening the meaning of responsibility. For this exploration, let it be asserted that responsibility emerges as the key when the following functional areas are examined.

Identity. Who really defines the clergyperson? From what sources and authority come the signs and symbols of one's status and role? What nonprofessional forces assume an identity for clergy and then function with those assumptions in relating to them?

Function. Who says what a clergyperson does? Where do job descriptions come from and what power do they have over ministerial performance? How does one know that one is doing the proper work of the ministerial profession?

Conditions. Who says when, where, and how the work of ministry is done? How is personal autonomy and institutional need negotiated? To what task, location, and role are clergy called, and who says so?

Education. Who decides what skills and specialized knowledge are essential for admission to professional practice? Who says what continuing education is necessary for practitioners' growth and development?

The New Shape of Ministry

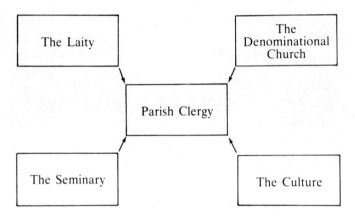

Maturation. Who decides whether or not one is developing competence? Who defines success for the profession? Who acknowledges the continuity of a lifelong vocation and is concerned with career patterns and critical junctures of change within a lifetime of work?

Authority. Who is really in charge, who calls the shots? Who answers these questions?

These are six lenses that magnify the subject of our analysis. They will help us isolate an answer to the question of where responsibility lies for the ministerial profession. I do have one answer to this question that is shocking and surprising, which we will come to in due course. For now, let us proceed to name some of the factors that shape ministerial life and practice, especially those that are amenable to change.

Components of the Church Affecting the Parish Clergy

The diagram on the following page identifies four components which directly impinge upon the ministerial profession. My purpose here is not just to name these mighty factors, but to describe and evaluate their effect. Their impact upon the ministerial profession can be changed.

The Seminary

Description. The seminary is an integral component in the shaping of ministry. It has become a graduate school in relatively recent history, growing from the curriculum of a college or university into a specialized school similar to those in medicine and law. Usually, a bachelor's degree from an accredited college is a prerequisite for admission. Seminary education is normally a three-year course of study resulting in a Master of Divinity degree. Increasingly, seminaries offer a professional degree at the doctoral level. Curricula have considerable variety, but almost all seminaries offer studies in the traditional areas of Bible, church history, and theology. Beyond these there is a wide-ranging choice of electives and requirements. Each seminary has its own ethos, and consequently special emphases and styles emerge in the ministerial profession. There is also considerable latitude in the mix of academic and practicum courses in preparation for professional conduct. There is definitely no uniform pattern of integrating clinical experience (field work) and academic discipline. The current patterns range from intensive contextual education to no connection at all between church and seminary.

Today, seminaries are experiencing a crisis. And this is nothing new, they are always in crisis! But, to make a value judgment, this is good because they are living amidst the special tension of faith and culture. That tension is the dynamism of theological education. There is a constant in the flux of theological education and that is the insistence by the seminaries that they do not admit persons to the practice of the profession. This is a prerogative of the church. Seminaries only certify that an individual has fulfilled the academic requirements for a recognized degree.

Despite the self-imposed limitation, the seminary is an important factor in shaping ministerial roles and functions. In the first place, most churches which confer ordination upon individuals, thereby admitting them to professional practice, require graduation from an accredited seminary as one criterion for ordination. There are a few exceptions to this practice, but the general rule is: no diploma, no ordination. So, in effect, the self-imposed boundary that limits the scope of the seminary is murky. As far as I know, church groups do not intrude upon the curricular prerogatives of the seminary. The notorious uproar at Concordia Seminary of the Missouri Synod Lutheran Church in St. Louis comes to mind as an example of the fallout which precipitates when church bodies do interfere with academic freedom. And, in practical matters, seminaries also have great autonomy about whom they admit, what they require, and what they teach.

But, practical matters aside, by its very nature theological education is a potent factor in shaping the ministerial profession. For what we learn and the way we are taught set abiding patterns in each of us. Theological education at its best just whets the appetite for a lifelong questing after truth through disciplined, intellectual inquiry. Every practicing clergyperson owes an enormous debt of gratitude to his or her seminary.

Clergy grouse and complain about seminaries. "They never taught me that in seminary!" is a familiar war cry. Seminary faculties and administrations take a lot of abuse from professionals, most of it undeserved and unwelcomed. But despite the grousing, clergy have both a dependency on and an affection for schools of theology. My contention is that much of who we are and what we do is directly related to our experiences in seminary.

One cannot overstate the impact of theological education upon the practice of the profession, nor can one ignore the relationship of the seminary to the continuing education of the church professional.

Critique. At the risk of sounding like one of the complainers, I nevertheless wish to advance a critique of the seminaries *vis-à-vis* the profession. This critique is not about curriculum nor teaching competency (although I have been known to hold forth on such matters), it has to do with role models. Theological education is putting forth the wrong role models for fledgling clergy. In a word, its role model is academic, not professional.

By its very nature ministerial work is collaborative, not individual. In the practice of ministry the greatest brain in the world is doomed to failure if that brain is not encased in a person with relational skills. As practitioners, we rise and fall not by our individual excellence, but by our interpersonal ministries within a community of faith. Why, then, do seminaries persist in using grades and other individualistic models of achievement? Instead of individual grades, why not give a class grade to measure group dynamics—how did we do as a group? This would be far more akin to the performance measurements that are significant for parish clergy.

In skill areas also, the academic pattern prevails over the professional model. Your personal experience and mine, too, confirms this. After spending nineteen years in the school system, do you know what I was good at? I was good at the school system. I knew how to write term papers, how to listen to lectures, how to speak the jargon. I did not graduate from seminary as a professional, I graduated as a miniprofessor—and not a very good one at that! My sermons were lectures; I read books late at night and slept late in the morning; I thought ministry was hard and confining work, but no one ever asked me to write a term paper!

Now, you may think this critique is building to a knockout blow on the seminaries' jaw, but you will be surprised. I do not want to change what the seminaries do. I want to change what the clergy does with theological education. (I will elaborate on the methodology in the first advocacy under orientation to the practice.) At this point, I simply want to note the problem of the academic role model in theological education. One proof of the power of this model is the guilt that clergy articulate about not having enough time to read and write. Wherever do they get such an expectation of their role? You probably know where it comes from and how powerful it is.

Who affects our identity and function? The seminaries do.

The Laity

Description. The Social Security system classifies clergy as self-employed. If ever one doubted that bureaucracies are looney, this proves it! Clergy are group-employed, but there is no bureaucratic category for this. The clergy, being a minority group within the congregation, hardly count; we are outnumbered about two hundred to one. Looked at crassly (and erroneously), the laity pay our salaries, hire and fire us, and give us our strokes and lashes. Clergy spend far more time with laity than with their peers.

What other profession is most analogous to the ministry? Law, medicine, and theology were the classical professions, and it is sometimes assumed that the ministry is like the legal or medical profession. But that certainly is not true functionally. Doctors and lawyers have entrepreneurial relationships with clients. They are paid for their advice and treatment. They succeed or fail according to the efficacy of their treatment or the soundness of their advice as it affects the lives and well-being of their clients. Nothing like that is true of parish clergy. The profession most like ours is politics. Before you throw this book across the room, hear me out. In the political profession there are hacks as well as statesmen. Both must relate to a constituency. But the hack simply knows how to live off his constituency. He knows when to speak up and when to keep still, where to push and where to pull. All his effort is directed toward holding his constituents so that they will return him to office year after year. The statesman also has

31

a constituency which he must serve or he too will be out of office. He cannot always depart from his constituency or they will reject his leadership, but, on the other hand, the statesman sees the larger issues and movements of history. His task is knowing where people are and where they ought to be and how to move them. His best tool is persuasion.

The same situation applies to the conduct of parish ministry. Clergy relate to a lay constituency. If one does not like the way lay people think or act and does not welcome the challenge of moving them from where they are to where one thinks they ought to be, one might consider becoming a shoe salesperson. We clergy live and work amidst the tension between the aspirations and realities of the church. Those who lose either their vision or their compassion should not stay in the pastorate.

Clergy often make assumptions about the laity. It is a grievous mistake for them to assume that laypersons know who the clergy are, how they got to be that way, what they do, and why they ought to do it. Most serious ruptures between clergy and laity have their root in a lack of understanding about ministerial and lay roles. The fault for that lack of understanding is almost always the clergy's. They have forgotten to keep in touch with their constituencies.

Given this analysis of the enormous power that the lay constituency has over clergy in matters crass and profound, does it not seem prudent for clergy to just mind the store, keep their noses to the parish grindstones, and stay away from peer involvements? Who needs them, when all the honey is in the laity's hive? This is precisely how hacks emerge in the ministerial profession.

Keynote: Who Is Responsible for the Parish Clergy?

Critique. The problem of the lay constituency and its enormous power over the profession is not that it demands too much from the clergy. Quite the contrary, the problem is that laity expect too little because they know too little. If lay persons had all the skills necessary for effective church leadership there would be no need for clergy. The simple fact is that they are not skilled, and that is why the church has clergy. But sometimes overlooked within that little syllogism is the proposition that those who are inadequate to lead themselves can still be in positions of supervision over those who profess to lead them.

You clergy may not welcome this surprising paragraph, but I must write it. The laity are letting the clergy off because they understand far too little of what constitutes effective ministry. The laity see that the clergy are very busy, but never think to ask their leaders what they are busy doing, whether they are doing the right things, or whether they are doing them well. The laity simply do not ask the questions or know the answers. When you ask them, which is what happens in the review process of most pastor/parish committees, you will find that they are using inadequate indices to measure your performance. If people are coming to church and have not boycotted *en masse* then you must be doing all right. Suppose you were even preaching from the Koran, no one would call you to task if you just dressed it up a bit. And in matters important to your working conditions, the standard of measurement is almost always what others are doing. (That's how the whole system impinges upon you and your performance.) The laity tend to value institutional survival and the priestly functions. Attend to these matters alone and you will have no trouble with your constituency. You will also be a professional hack.

Before leaving this critique let's take a walk on the other side of the street. Clergy who are in deep trouble with their constituencies are not necessarily prophets, they may simply have ignored the other half of the proposition: keeping in touch. Furthermore, some of the best and most enduring insights that I have into the purpose and mission of the church, I owe not to great theologians, but to those in the pews who care about their church and its ministry.

In a critique of this sort one cannot do justice to all the subtleties and ambiguities. I bow my head in gratitude to the many fine lay people who have loved and helped me, but I will stick to my basic insight: the laity tend to be too easy on the clergy. I believe there is an intermediate stratum for pastor/parish relationships, one where more insightful supervision and review can be given. The details of that will emerge as the advocacies unfold, but for now simply comprehend the enormous authority of the laity over the clergy and the *un*discerning way it is exercised.

The Denominational Church

Description. The great idea of our time is ecumenism, a new day for interchurch relationships. But in euphoria over the new day, never forget that the old one fades slowly. We are still a divided Christendom. We are enclaves of faith and practice, of custom and tradition. The existential strain of this moment in our history is that conceptualizations of faith are far ahead of institutional practices. It was necessary for me to introduce this book with an apology because in our day an interdenominational readership still poses problems of polity in a book on the ministerial profession. This may be cause for sadness but it is certainly a fact with which clergy and their advocates must come to grips.

Even those who give only lip service to their denominations are very much a part of these systems and the ways they shape the profession. This shaping is expressed in subtly diverse ways, but it is still the denomination that admits ministers into practice, that greatly influences parish placement, and that advances or retards careers.

In every hierarchical system there are inequities, and the denominational church has its share. I identified myself in the introduction as one well-served by the church system, but left unsaid whether I feel this way because of who I am or because the church system has been kind to me, or because I am comfortable with the givens of my polity. Clergy tend to be uncomfortable when the system does not work in their interest, and comfortable with it when it does. (You didn't know this was going to be a book about sin too, but there it is!)

Critique. It is very hard and may be quite foolish for clergy to be critical of the denominational church, not because we are intimidated by its hierarchies but because we are part of that structure. I know of no church polity that excludes the clergy from its machinery. I know of some that give the clergy disproportionate authority. So we have all had a hand in creating and maintaining whatever it is in the denominational church that affects us.

Strangely, my critique of the denominational church concerns not what it does, but what it prevents. Denominationalism prevents clergy from forming peer groups of substance. The denominations are all for cooperative efforts in such simple things as combined summer services with other communions and in more significant things such as shared mission strategies at home and abroad, and yet cooperation has not been extended to reciprocity of clergy. It is unthinkable that other denominations should participate in the key decisions of their peers. Would the Presbyterians allow an Episcopalian on their ordination committee? Would the Methodists consult the Lutherans about a pastoral appointment? Not on their lives they wouldn't. The prevention of such clergy participation in key moments keeps the denominational church relatively secure and the clergy from being accountable to their peers. This is not part of some malevolent design. I know of no conspirators who keep the clergy from taking counsel together. But I do know that the denominational church exercises enormous power over the parish clergy by holding fast to the key decisions of ordination and placement. The relinquishment of those two critical powers would be the end of the effect of denominationalism upon the clergy. Is that not what the Consultation on Church Union discovered?

I am not saying that the denominations should be disbanded, or even that they are enemies of the parish clergy. I am simply exploring who is responsible for the parish clergy, and the denominational church is certainly a mighty fortress when it comes to affecting the ministerial profession.

The Culture

Description. Culture is an all-inclusive term. It is the given environment of the church in the world. The ministerial profession is part of the culture. So are the seminaries, the laity, and the denominations. I have never subscribed to the easy demarcation of sacred and secular; it is hard to tell which is which. But this division has a useful, shorthand identification purpose, so let us use it. In this sense the culture is the whole of the nonconfessing world which refers to those outside the church who acknowledge its existence in its many forms and claims. Their number is legion, and their impact on the clergy is greater than you might expect.

When I meet a stranger on neutral ground, say in the seat next to me on an airplane or on the first tee at the golf course, we chat amicably until the conversation turns to my vocation. I become nervous and uncomfortable—it is a familiar moment for clergy. I know some who fabricate a career hoping that they will be acceptable to the stranger. I just hang my head, look down, and say meekly, "I'm a minister."

Why do we do such things? Are we embarrassed by our vocation? I am not, I am proud to be a part of it. It is not shame that makes me uncomfortable, it is something more pervasive than that. I know this stranger already has a lot of preconceptions about the clergy. Churchgoer or not, the culture has taught him how to act. He must clean up his language and his jokes in my presence. He must confess his own sympathies for religion. He must ask me if I knew Reverend So-and-So. I have been down this road with strangers many times, and I do not welcome the pilgrimage.

This anecdote discloses why culture is one of the factors that affect clergy. People think they know a lot about clergy. They see Billy Graham on television. They saw Bing Crosby in "Going My Way." They read Harry Kemelman mysteries. A Protestant, a Catholic, and a Jew; there they are for all the world to see, but not one of them is really me.

In the 1960s the culture suffered a terrible shock. There, in the demonstrations for racial justice and for peace in Vietnam—right there out in the streets, away from their pulpits and altars—were the clergy. The culture was not ready for this. People had not read Niebuhr and Bonhoeffer. People had their own expectations of the clergy, and were surprised by what they saw.

Not only do people presume to know our identities, they presume to know our value and our work. According to the culture clergy are poor, so give them a hand out; they can use the donation. And everybody knows that all successful clergy are in the bigger and better churches. In our culture bigness and success are Siamese twins. So according to this index, the minister really doing his job is the minister that really packs the pews. People think they know all there is to know about the clergy. But their cultural labels are unreal.

Critique. Cultural ignorance about clergy is easily documented and righteously lamented. But where did those ideas come from? Who lets the culture set the index for success in the profession? This is the heart of the matter, and the answer is sadly obvious: the clergy themselves. We have not bothered to change the image of the minister in the popular mind and in the mass media. On television, in the movies, or in a contemporary novel, when have you seen a minister portrayed as a thoughtful, human, and competent person? Such clergy do not exist in the mass media, yet they are all around us.

But more than an image is at stake here. Clergy themselves have been duped by the culture and this is most poignantly apparent in our quest for success. It is we who have succumbed to the imagery of the age when we think about our battles and our victories. We have allowed the hucksterism of the culture to permeate our churches, our professions, and still worse, our souls. The way the culture has affected the clergy may be the heaviest burden of all.

An Answer to the Question

In seeking to answer the question, Who is responsible for the parish clergy? we have named factors and forces that affect the clergy's identity, functions, conditions, education, maturation, and authority. Four powerful sources of influence have been identified: the seminaries, the laity, the denominations, and the culture. Each of these sources was described as impacting the profession and shaping and molding it according to their own assumptions. Next, the impact of each source was briefly criticized. As we look for what can be changed, it is important to know just what needs changing. Thus we have talked briefly about inappropriate role models, inept supervision, personnel control and indices of success.

Have we come, then, to an answer? Is the answer that an amalgam of four factors shapes, directs, and controls the ministerial profession? No, that is not the answer. These four factors are powerful. Singly and collectively they do make an impact. But they are not specifically *responsible* for the ministerial profession.

The correct answer to our question is that *no one is responsible for the parish clergy.* That's right! The seminaries are not responsible, the laity are not responsible, the denominations are not responsible, and the culture is not responsible. Clergy just like to think that they are. It is comfortable to have someone or something to blame for what makes us be what we are and do what we do. If you listen carefully to preacher-talk, you will often hear one of these four factors blamed for wreaking havoc in our lives.

THE problem lies with us. We do not take responsibility for our own profession. We have allowed a vacuum to develop which others rush to fill. We let others, not ourselves, define our identity. We let others, not ourselves, describe our functions. We let others define our educational needs, set the conditions of our services, and provide for our maturation. We have abdicated to others the responsibility for ourselves.

In the search for what can be changed an answer emerges: we can change. We can take more responsibility for our profession. It is not a given that we must abdicate to others the concepts of who we are and what we do.

But please do not bolt toward the finish line. Make sure you know where you are going, and why. Do not rush toward solidarity so that collectively you can throw out the mistaken masses. That would be disastrous. For we are parts of and partners with the seminaries, the laity, the denominations, and the culture. To attack these entities would be to assume that they are our enemies, when the enemy is our abdication of responsibility.

True, we do need to get together to assert ourselves and to fill the vacuum at the center of our own profession. But why must this be done? It must be done so that we can establish reciprocity with those other entities. We have been unequal partners, and in our inequality we have contributed to the confusion of the seminaries, the laity, the denominations, and the culture. There can be no dialogue when one party converses in scattered whispers. I have no illusion that we will ever speak with one voice. But I am convinced that clergy with a strong sense of responsibility for our profession will be welcomed into a partnership and that the whole church will be stronger for our acceptance of responsiblity.

First Steps

The intention of this book has now become clear: it is to change the attitudes, self-concepts, and performance of the clergy as these pertain to the profession. This will not happen quickly, it will be a long, laborious process. It will begin with a plan which has broad-based support. I do not have such a plan. All I have now are some planks on which to stand and survey the situation.

My intention is to stimulate your thinking about the task before us, in two ways. First, I want to set before you a series of advocacies, written in the form of resolutions which may be adopted, amended, or rejected by you as a member of the clergy. Each advocacy contains a proposition and then some background notes about how these matters currently function or dysfunction. Second, I have included guidelines for change by clergy who take

41

responsibility for their profession. Following these guidelines I offer organizational forms that may facilitate their enactment.

Here ends the keynote address. So let us begin the serious work of becoming responsible for our profession.

Agenda Item 1:
Orientation to the Practice

BE IT RESOLVED: That practitioners of the ministerial profession become responsible for the orientation of beginning parish clergy.

Background Notes on the Present System

There are critical moments in a lifetime. These are often times of transition, when the old has passed away and the new has not yet begun. For clergy, the first pastorate is such a moment. It is especially critical because it includes life with strangers in a new location and in a new home, to say nothing of forsaking old school patterns and beginning new professional patterns. At this critical juncture the patterns of life, attitudes of thought, and conceptions of the church and its ministry are likely to make an enduring impression.

Where are our peers in the profession during these critical moments?

The Person and the Process

There are many paths to the ministerial profession. Personality types grow from different origins and follow different time sequences toward the point where they begin in earnest the practice of ministry. Sometimes entry begins in midlife, as a colleague in a multiple-staff church. But let me describe the normal pattern and allow you to redefine it in terms of your individual circumstances.

Paul S. shows promise for ministerial leadership while in the youth group at his church. He is intelligent, thoughtful of others, and has been nurtured in the church since birth. Paul expresses a willingness to explore the ministry as his vocation in life. Both his family and pastor support him. His pastor urges him to proceed with a solid liberal arts education in college. He does so and finds God's truth in all of life—the arts, history, the sciences. An urging within him leads him to discover more of God's truth and to devote his life in God's service. He attends an excellent seminary, where he matures in the disciplines of religious thought. Assured of graduation, he meets with the denomination's committee on ordination and learns what he must do. He then meets with the denomination's regional executive and learns of job opportunities. So he meets with the pastoral committees of local churches. A call to be pastor of Great Prairie View Church is extended. And so he begins his professional work as a parish minister.

Agenda Item 1: Orientation to the Practice

This is the pattern that masquerades as orientation to the pastorate in many of our lives. It is what happened to me, and I suspect is recognizable to you as a typical pattern. That is the way we did it, and look how well we turned out. What is wrong with that pattern?

Much is wrong. Its model is not one of orientation to a profession, but is based on survival of the fittest. Aren't we the humane, people-centered profession? We are partners in an institution that cares about people and intentionally provides for their growth and development, right? Of course that is right, but why don't we put this into practice with the beginner?

Almost immediately the beginner is confronted with three powerful forces in the church system: the seminary, the denominational church, and the laity. He (or she) is one single person, confronting three separate church systems. Furthermore, each system is asking of this person something different from the other, and I am reasonably sure that the three entities have not talked with one another about the process and how it impinges upon the individual making the passage. I predict that within two years that young man will: (a) be back at the seminary for more education; (b) be seeking another church somewhere else; (c) have left the profession or wished he had never begun.

I do not want to be overly dramatic. We must be doing something right—the defection rate is not all that great. Besides, every other profession has the same "ordeal by fire" initiation. But just because many of us began our professional life that way does not mean that subsequent initiates must do the same. You would think we would know better, that we had learned from our own experience.

However, chances are that what we remember is not the agony of passage, but the saints of the church who came to our rescue. In fact, they may not have been great saints at all, but they came upon us in a time of great need and seemed saintly because they took the time to care about our growth.

The present pattern of survival of the fittest practically guarantees the formation of another generation of clergy indifferent to a collegial style. The longer we establish beginners through a pattern of individualistic performance, the longer we will have individuals at odds with the church system.

Understanding the Problem

Beginning pastors have some difficult problems. For most of their lives they have been students. Now they cease being students and become practitioners. Further, in my previous discussion of the impact of the seminary on the profession I noted the role models by which the seminary trains its students. Just as I did, new clergy will persist in being miniprofessors until they discover that this does not work in Great Prairie View Church. Through academia they have whet their appetites for the higher offerings of life. How many symphonies are there in Great Prairie View?

The church system introduces itself to the beginner in disjointed components. The seminary wants intellectual acumen. The denomination wants adherence to the order of the church. The laity want a pastor who will solve the problems of Great Prairie View Church which have accumulated for years. Each of these claims upon a person is apppropriate, but considering his or her limited experience they all seem to cascade upon the new pastor at once, without design or communication. The claims are part of a pattern, but the fledgling pastor may be dismayed when all these demands are compressed into a short span of time, causing them to seem disjointed and sometimes in conflict. The new pastor often feels he or she is being torn apart.

For those who begin in this pattern frustration and isolation are likely companions. How long they will plague the beginner is uncertain, but I think it unnecessary that they be there at all. In times like these one needs pastoral friends, not frustration and isolation.

Consider an Alternative

That pattern of orientation need not persist. It does so because present practitioners are not intentional about the orientation of beginning clergy. That scenario is a single example of what happens when there is a vacuum instead of aggressive responsibility on the part of professional colleagues. Consider a possibility for change.

Clergy could function as professional tutors. Let us assume that a group of clergy decided to become responsible for the orientation of beginning pastors. How would such a commitment operate?

First, in order to alleviate the disjointedness of the church system, these professional tutors would have to make a long-term commitment to the seminarians. For the purpose of discussion let us say four years, the last two years of seminary and the first two years of the pastorate.

The actual process begins with rapport building in which

current practitioners and current students come to know each other as persons. Also during the seminary years the tutors, the seminary personnel, and the students gather for a periodic progress review. As a student's education progresses, the tutor begins to make contacts on the student's behalf with the denominational machinery. Ordination and placement should be planned with the denomination long before the last few months of seminary. And in the last year of seminary, the tutor could help the student immeasurably by initiating some simulated parish experiences. An evening with laypersons acting as a pastoral search committee could simulate the interview process, thus providing the experience of being interviewed, without the pressure of actually seeking a position. The same kind of simulation could be done with groups of clergy and lay people to simulate the ordination examination. As the real ordination and placement begin I suspect the overseers for both events would welcome the evaluation of the tutor who hs come to know the candidate as a person.

If geography permits, it would be good for the progessional tutor to stay close at hand for the newcomer's beginning parish practice. Most certainly, help could be given with planning ahead, managing one's time (a great problem for beginning clergy who have been students all their lives), and carrying out the details of consultations about priestly functions which may be known in theory but not in practice—for instance, What do you do at a wedding rehearsal? Practicing professionals have mountains of information that would benefit beginners: things like how to read a church budget, how to deal with the emotional cripples who come to see the new pastor in town, and where to send for various program aids. It is astonishing how little information beginners have, and even more astonishing how little is passed from one professional to another.

All the time this guidance is taking place something far more important is happening. The beginner is gaining an authentic role model in his profession. He is experiencing the presence of one who has learned his craft and functions within the church systems. If this pattern were just to begin it probably would be self-perpetuating—one generation almost automatically would do it for another.

This is what can happen if practitioners assume responsibility for the orientation of beginners. To be sure, there are many obstacles to easy enactment. Beginners are often brash and arrogant. They do not take quickly to older professionals. Similarly, practicing professionals are intimidated by the young with their fresh, new knowledge. This suggestion then involves a two-sided threat. Indeed, it may be that just such a threat is what has kept beginners and practitioners apart. But the collegial benefits are also two-sided. The entire profession is strengthened when bridges are built and crossed by practitioners within the profession.

There are other, more complicated, alternatives to the orientation of beginning professionals by experienced colleagues. I cannot understand why the concept of "teaching churches" has not gained wider use. Where they have been used the results have been beneficial. This concept calls for a partnership between the clergy, laity, seminary, and denomination. A student simultaneously begins his or her seminary education with an internship in a local church. The student attends classes at seminary, but lives and works at the nearby teaching church. Thus, during the seminary years one is also learning about professional matters with a congregation that acts intentionally as a teaching church.

If this seems unworkable, some small local churches could specialize as beginner-pastorates. These churches will expect short-term tenure and less than polished leadership. But they can also say that their specialty in mission is to help recent seminary graduates become better ministers.

Of course, if I had a magic wand and could change the whole system, I would do so. My wand would create a system which made full use of apprenticeship opportunities. I would alter the sequence by breaking up the simultaneity of the present system. First, there would be a seminary course, to study the classical disciplines; then, there would be two years of supervised apprenticeship with an experienced professional in a local church; and after that, a year back at the seminary to take electives in skill areas that need development. After all these experiences would come ordination and the beginning of a first pastorate.

This may seem a highly unlikely alternative, but it is helpful to build models of how things might be done if we were more intentional about orienting new pastors to the profession.

A Review of the Issues

For the most part clergy have abandoned the task of orienting beginning professionals into the practice of ministry. (John Wesley advised new pastors to live in the homes of experienced ministers.) This abandonment has resulted in stronger influences from the seminary, the denominational church, and the laity which are neither desirable for these parts of the church system nor for the beginners themselves. Then, too, individual achievement is the predominant pattern in the seminary, and shortly becomes the predominant pattern in the first pastorate. Both are contrary to intentional collegiality.

Present practitioners can seize the initiative in establishing a new partnership with the seminary, denominational church, and laity to form a caring ministerial profession. The specific forms for doing this are not as important as the desire for that partnership to be established. As in art, form will follow function. I leave you with the question: Will the current practitioners of a profession seeking to be responsible for itself take on the task of orienting newcomers into its ranks?

Agenda Item 2:
Defining Success

BE IT RESOLVED: That parish clergy define success for themselves.

Background Notes on the Present System

Clergy are both lured and repelled by success. Wrestling with the definition of success is seen as an intrusion upon the basic conceptions of the profession. Our theological inclinations are to substitute other, preferred, goals for our lives. Terms like faithfulness, commitment, and sacrifice are more congenial to our mind-set and lifestyle. The intruding of pressures for success in our minds and lives comes from the culture and is the price we pay for living in this time and place. The current method of dealing with questions about success has been to ignore them, to refuse to wrestle with them, and to substitute other, more biblical, goals for success. But avoidance has not produced resolution, it has produced aberrations among practitioners of the profession. This advocacy does not put forth a definition of success, but is an invitation to join with your colleagues in defining for yourselves the issues that surround success.

Before the wrestling begins it might be helpful to choose sides and establish the rules of the match. I propose that the issues be divided into personal and professional. Both obviously reside in one whole person, but I think we gain clarification about the subject if we separate the two. As my personal goals of success I am satisfied to hold the rich biblical concepts of faithfulness, commitment, and sacrifice. To be sure, there are still questions of substance and implication clustered around these concepts. Meanings are personal. We bring our own special meanings to these terms and act upon them accordingly. On the other side, there are professional goals with collective and collaborative definitions for the whole practice of parish ministry. This is the substance of the second advocacy.

Although I am dividing personal and professional issues into two sides for clarification, they are in fact interrelated. Your professional goals of success are what you achieve in fulfilling your personal goals; if you do not have the former you will never achieve the latter. Conversely, professional definitions of success will shrivel if they are not rooted in well-conceived personal goals.

The rules of the wrestling match are the foundations of

this agenda. We are trying intentionally as a profession to pursue collective understandings of success.

The Person and the Process

Career crises emerge at predictable points in a lifetime. Each person will come upon these moments whatever his path, and each will resolve the crises in ways appropriate to his or her personality and situation. Consider this one example as representative of a wide range of vocational crises.

Matthew T. is thirty-nine years old, father of two, and pastor of Grace Church in a middle-sized city. The morning mail has brought him a letter informing him that he has been suggested as a candidate for a pastoral vacancy at Hope Church. Would he be willing to meet with the pastoral search committee? Matthew T. ponders the invitation.

This would be his fourth move in the fifteen years since his ordination. He knows his family would be reluctant to move again. He also knows that Hope Church has a larger membership than Grace Church, and presumably offers a larger salary and more challenge. He is very much attracted by these prospects. It is time to get serious about providing the funds for the kids' college education; he cannot see how the present family resources will be able to take on college bills without a higher income.

He muses over the past five years at Grace Church. He thinks he has done about all he can in this place. The church needs a change of leadership, and he needs a new challenge. He senses stagnation in his own growth, that he has been coasting for the past two years. In short, he is

55

bored—although he never uses that word. He is flattered that Hope Church has expressed an interest in him because he knows there are very few vacancies these days.

He turns to the typewriter and writes three hundred words of pious palaver that say yes.

The thought may never occur to him, but Matthew T. has a success problem. Neither he personally nor his colleagues collectively have wrestled with this issue. He sees success as a problem of salespeople and executives and is relieved because he thinks that's one problem he needn't worry about. But now outside pressures have intruded. He wants to be a good provider for his family, and he thinks that the way to improve those provisions is to change pastorates. He also knows that parish clergy have an "itinerant" heritage. Some of his ancestors in the profession were circuit riders. Of course, they were in a frontier culture and not a settled-down culture, but the image still remains. Matthew T. has avoided the question of success and in that avoidance has allowed an aberration to settle the question for him.

Let me state a fact and offer an interpretation. The fact is that clergy move a lot. There is indisputable evidence. (On the staff of my professional journal for clergy one person was employed just to keep track of changes of address!) I know that America is a mobile, nomadic country. I also know that one of the givens in the profession is "shake the dust off your feet" and move on to the next church. There are professional considerations for doing this, and for doing it as often as the clergy surplus will allow.

But there are other aspects of the moving syndrome.

Agenda Item 2: Defining Success

Frequent moves are very expensive for the church and for the clergy. A higher salary is often eaten up by new draperies for the manse and increased options for spending disposable cash. Churches require trust relationships with their pastors. If a church has had four pastors in twenty years it has spent about ten years just building trust relationships before it can get on with its mission. In short, the congregation has wasted half its time, money, and energy accommodating itinerant clergy. I have no data, but I suspect the collective cost in terms of lost revenues and moving expenses could be counted annually in the millions of dollars! This is a luxury the church system can ill afford.

In neglecting to challenge the moving syndrome, as a definition of success, the profession pays a high price. James Glasse, president of Lancaster Theological Seminary, spotlights the problem with some anecdotes in *Profession: Minister* wherein he wryly translates preacher-talk. He observes that preachers often say to fellow preachers, "I have been at this church five years. I think I have done all the good I can do here." Other preachers then nod their heads in sagacious agreement. Glasse asks himself: Does a doctor say, "I have been here five years. I have healed all the sick I can heal"? Does a lawyer say, "I have been here five years. I have won about all the cases I can win"? Of course not. Preacher-talk does not translate to other professions. Maybe it's because other professions have done a better job of defining success for themselves. Glasse concludes with several truthful zingers: "If a minister says he has had fifteen years' experience, what he means is that he has had five years' experience three times over." And, "If a minister keeps moving, the only thing he really has to change is his address!"

Thus the moving syndrome continues unchallenged. It becomes a substitute for growth. It becomes a substitute for progress. It becomes a substitute for fulfillment. It is a poor—and expensive—substitute for success.

Understanding the Problem

The problem is avoidance. Clergy act out their personal goals, but will not deal with their professional goals.

In the question of professional success, I think the problem is hidden in conceptualization. The church system conceives of ministry almost exclusively in terms of a pastor/parish relationship, and I have no quarrel with the importance of that concept. But where do career patterns come in? Maybe the problem can be clarified in terms of a horizontal/vertical image. The model of relationship between a pastor and a congregation is expressed horizontally, but career patterns are expressed vertically, beginning with ordination and ending with disengagement. Clergy have been resolving the vertical dimension of their career patterns by moving into new horizontal relationships, which they hope are higher on the vertical scale.

This is a problem because of the vacuum in the ministerial profession. The church system, which expresses itself best through horizontal relationships, really has no plan for ministerial careers. Why should it? It is the ministers, not the church system, who have a need for career patterns. But we ministers keep silent about professional success, the issue goes unanswered, and the moving syndrome continues.

Agenda Item 2: Defining Success

Consider an Alternative

I said at the beginning that I could not define success, but I hope the preceding ideas have helped you review the issues. I claim to know an approach for resolving the issue of success. Basically, it requires the profession to be more intentional about career patterns. The profession cannot expect much help from the laity of the denominational church on these matters. This is an instance where ministers must be responsible for themselves.

I have tried many times to chart a normative career pattern for clergy, starting with age demarcations on the left side and church situations at the bottom. But when I begin to depict and project that pattern, matching age and situation, I tear up the graph and throw it away, saying it is too complicated and that there are too many variables to plot. But this is only partly true. The real truth is that I do not want to be pigeonholed. My life simply cannot be reduced to lines on a chart. Nevertheless, the exercise is worthwhile, and I recommend it to you for the learning which results from attempting to plot out your life.

As an approach to defining success let me share what I have learned from futilely trying to graph my life! The best approach is not to plot one's whole career. Break it into manageable pieces, and work with just one piece at a time. One does need to conceptualize the whole pattern, what I call the vertical dimension of a lifetime in the profession, but consider it and then lay it aside.

You may divide your career into as many smaller segments as you wish. For simplicity I used just three: the period of preparation and adjustment, the period of creativity, and the period of assimilation and disengagement. Both the number and the titles are highly arbitrary. What is not arbitrary is the concept of looking at the pieces instead of the whole.

For each title I began to write growth goals: What do I expect to learn, to do, to offer, to receive in each of these periods? I also added an anticipatory statement: What do I now need to be doing that will begin to prepare me for what comes next?

Having described my growth goals, I added some resource ideas in adjacent columns. Who will help me do that? Where can this best be accomplished? Are there any sequences I should note here—does one thing come logically after another?

Finally, I began to project a church that would best suit my growth and resource needs. Churches do come in types and it is possible to categorize them. If church management, for instance, emerges as a specialty in my creative period, I would not want to look to a 200-member rural congregation for that specialty.

I commend this process to you. Of course, it has many deficiencies. Placement is a major obstacle. One's own maturation or shifting value structure is another. However, by so charting one's goals, one begins to think about success not in great and grandiose forms, but in smaller, more manageable units. One begins to build bridges between professional career needs and local church pastor/parish relationships.

A Review of the Issues

The issue of success is one of the few instances where the

church system is in conflict with the profession. In my opinion the profession has acquiesced to the church system. But the church system is paying a price for its dominance, a price in terms of the frequent moves which undo the trust patterns necessary for effective mission.

The real reason success is a problem for everyone, but especially for clergy, lies in the problem of measurement. How will you know when you have been successful? Other vocations can translate measurement into numbers. There are quotas, or dollars, or titles. We sometimes use titles and numbers as if they were objective data about our success. Hence the bigger and better church syndrome.

The alternative I have proposed for the parish clergy is the equivalent of numerical qualification. It invites practitioners to fill in their own quotas or goals. When one's goal has been reached one can be called successful.

Agenda Item 3:
Continuing Education

BE IT RESOLVED: That parish clergy seize the initiative in procuring the education they need for growth.

Background Notes on the Present System

Continuing education is revered among some parish clergy, but their number is not great. It is not for lack of offerings, indeed there is a plethora of courses, seminars, institutes, and books for ministers. But despite the bounty from the fertile fields of continuing education opportunities, the sad fact is that there are relatively few partakers.

Image is not a problem because clergy view themselves as a learned profession. Even though the idea of a learned ministry was conceived and pursued in a social order quite different from ours, that image is held high in our self-concepts. It is a puzzle, then, why continuing education is not well-supported by present practitioners. Is the problem the clergy or the education, or both?

The Person and the Process

Mary V. is in a bad mood as she enters her office to begin the day. She has not slept well after last night's trustees' meeting. She never enjoys the meetings and last night was a case in point. The task was to cut the budget, for the trustees insisted on a balanced budget. Mary V. was sure that the resources for meeting the proposed budget were available, but the trustees looked only at the figures before them and proceeded to cut and slice. One of Mary's pet projects was sliced to shreds. "What do those stupid trustees know about the needs of senior citizens? They cut out all the funding for their day trips." That had made her mad; she was displeased with herself and in a grouchy mood.

She picked up the morning mail. Three letters (all bulk rate) were in the mailbox. With halfhearted interest she ripped open the first one. It was from a minister in California who wanted her to attend one of his church growth conferences. Included in the letter was a series of rave testimonials about how this conference had "doubled the size of many congregations." She quickly calculated that the tuition and airfare to California would cost more than her senior citizens' project. The next piece of mail was from her seminary, so she gave it some attention. Her dear alma mater announced a Ministers' Week Convocation on The

Agenda Item 3: Continuing Education

Feminine Presence in the Church. "Not much new ground
for me," she thought, "I *am* the feminine presence in this
church! The seminary should have a week for Trustees
Who Need Elementary Christianity," she mused. The third
piece of mail was the mimeographed newsletter from her
denominational judicatory. "*News*-letter," she thought,
"that's a laugh! Not much news here, just the usual
promotional stuff: a workshop on prayer and meditation, a
one-day conference on world hunger (bring a brown-bag
lunch), and a reminder about the minister's fall retreat." All
the letters went into the wastebasket as unacceptable.

Someday, she promised herself, I've got to do
something about my continuing education.

The case of Mary V. is not unique. The postage alone
(even bulk rate) spent to advertise continuing education
opportunities would feed a small nation for a week. We are
not exactly bereft of opportunities. It is a curious situation.
On the one hand, clergy believe in the importance of
continuing education, but do not support it in great
numbers. On the other hand, there are more opportunities
than any one minister could possibly attend, but most of the
offerings are being rejected. In either case, not much
continuing education is undertaken. How come?

Let me begin musing about this situation by making a
confession from my own experience. In the early days of my
ministry I went to many continuing education events,
especially those that were subsidized. I thought I went to
establish professional discipline—the learned ministry lives
on through me, and all that sort of business. But I confess
that I was bored by the continuing education that was

offered. Somehow it did not fit me. I kept going out of duty, but I noticed that the part of the experience that I liked best were the break times when I could talk with my colleagues, who, in those beginning days of isolation, I did not see very often. The camaraderie made the day worthwhile. This is an embarrassing confession, yet in those early days the small seed of an important insight was taking root.

The insight that was aborning in those early days grew and flowered as I came to understand the church system better. I began to realize that much of what is being offered in continuing education comes from someone else's agenda. Opportunities in continuing education are not given for the clergy, they are given for the sponsoring agency. Someone else has something they want me to know. A seminary wants to teach what it is able to teach. An institute wants to teach its specialty. A denominational judicatory wants to teach what it thinks I need to know.

Parish clergy consume what someone else has produced for them to attend, purchase, or learn. I hasten to add that sometimes this is not altogether bad. I have consumed some fine offerings that I would not have thought of, and they touched me when I needed a new direction. But it is a chancy process. Maybe an offering is what I need, and maybe it is what someone else thinks I need.

We are beginning to solve our puzzling situation. The substance of continuing ministerial education is not oriented to our needs, and we the consumers are saying "No, thanks" in great numbers. The system of continuing education is serving itself, and not the constituency it purports to serve.

Understanding the Problem

Part of the problem, then, is that parish clergy are not well-served by the system of continuing education. But that is only part of the problem. The other part is that the clergy have acquiesced to the system of continuing education.

Jim Glasse has another anecdote to illustrate the problem. He relates that one day a janitor at Vanderbilt Divinity School came into his office to do a small custodial chore. As the janitor worked they talked. He mentioned being tired that day. "Why?" asked Glasse. "Oh," he said, "I was up late last night. A bunch of us janitors here at the school got together to learn how to service our air-conditioning system." Exit the janitor, and Jim Glasse asked himself: "When was the last time I heard of a group of clergy getting together and paying someone to come in and teach them a skill they needed to know?" He could not remember it ever happening.

That spotlights the problem. Clergy do not feel responsible for their own education. They are takers, not seekers. Sometimes they even feel guilty about not taking enough. Yet they never seem to feel guilty about not getting what they need.

Take the case of Mary V. cited above. She turned down three opportunities. Why? Because they were not what *she* needed for professional growth. But Mary V. also ignored a very important piece of data. In her morning gloom, she was angry about the trustees' meeting. She felt inadequate compared to the hardheaded business types on the board. They knew so much more about budgets than she did. In her musings she wished the seminary would teach church

67

trustees how to be *church* trustees. Good idea. But a better idea would be for Mary to learn more about budgets and church finances herself.

Two things are needed to give Mary's story a happy ending. She needs to find out if there are any other clergy nearby who have a similar educational need. In this particular instance I would predict there are many. Then that group can pool its resources and purchase the services of someone who can teach them what they need to know. In carrying out this advocacy, I hope Mary and the others in her group do not try to purchase their education from some quasi-religious agency that pretends to offer what they want. I hope they find an accountant, one who may or may not give a rap for the church, but who knows how to make numbers meaningful. That is what they need to know, and the way to learn what they need to know.

Consider an Alternative

The advocacy here is for parish clergy to seize the initiative in procuring their own continuing education.

Church consultant Lyle Schaller has a dramatic idea. It does not stand a chance of enactment, but its citation here serves to focus our attention on an alternative. Schaller says that denominational judicatories should not contribute a single penny to subsidize continuing education. Instead, they should use a voucher plan. Let every pastor in the judicatory have a voucher worth so much to purchase whatever continuing education they think they need. Nice try, Lyle, but it will never fly!

It will never fly because it upsets the whole system of continuing education. It forces the system to become consumer oriented. The seminaries would hate it. The denominations would hate it. All the agencies with their specialties would hate it. Only the clergy would like it. They could get whatever they thought they needed. I suspect the demand for those vouchers would be so great that denominations would go bankrupt.

The Schaller Voucher Plan is given for illustrative purposes. It is not a viable alternative, but it points toward one that is. Remember my earlier confession about being bored with continuing education? I said I kept on attending because I enjoyed the camaraderie of my professional peers. Building on that insight, you'll find your colleagues make terrific learning partners. You may even have some things to teach each other. You may have common learning needs. If necessary, you can pool your finances to procure your own education. You can enjoy camaraderie while learning new skills. This is the style I advocate. The alternative to consuming what is offered is seizing the initiative and collectively procuring what you want.

In many ways, clergy's passivity regarding continuing education is the consequence of the role models followed in seminary. Passivity, in the face of one's educational needs, is a mark of immaturity toward one's professional development. The bridge from student to professional has not been crossed. The profession will come of age when it asserts its needs for continuing education upon the systems that deliver these services.

A Review of the Issues

This advocacy may sound critical of those who offer continuing education. But the fault does not lie with the purveyors of continuing education for clergy. I would not for a moment deter them from doing what they do best.

We began by asking why continuing education, which is purported to be highly desirable, is not widely supported. The insight we have arrived at here is not that present offerings are *ipso facto* bad or wrong, but that so much good continuing education is going unutilized because of a systemic problem implied in the keynote's central thrust: at the center of the forces affecting the ministerial profession there is a vacuum. The clergy themselves have abdicated responsibility for their professional development.

I genuinely believe that if clergy would ever own their profession, not only would there be more continuing education, but also a new and very creative partnership between the profession and those who help it grow.

Agenda Item 4:
Salaries

BE IT RESOLVED: That parish clergy be paid higher salaries.

Background Notes on the Present System

Clergy salaries are low in relation to contemporary norms. They always have been. One should not enter the profession for monetary reasons, nor should one stay in the profession for its financial compensations. But low salaries have personal and professional consequences that affect the function and nature of church professionals. It is conceivable that the parish ministry will become an avocation instead of a vocation if church salaries continue to plummet in relation to the others in the culture.

Salaries for the profession are low partly because clergy lack sophistication about money in general, and about their own salaries in particular. Many take biblical phrases such as, "the love of money is the root of evil" quite literally and do not understand money as a symbol of love and esteem. We are so much a part of an affluent society that we scarcely discern its ramifications. Even our extended period of educational preparation is a consequence of our affluence. In most cultures the young enter the labor force very early; we delay entry because we are so rich. An affluent culture is one of choices. We have multiple ways to earn money and to spend money. The love of money may indeed produce great evil, but money may also enable good choices, representing the enactment and development of our desires and goals. At the very least, let us say that clergy are ambivalent about money. They feel confused because money is a symbol of power. It can be used for good or evil, but either way it is an instrument of power.

Thus, this part of the agenda is about salaries, but it is also about power, values, and the way the profession deals or does not deal with these issues.

The Person and the Process

Mark C. was having a leisurely second cup of coffee with his wife after the children had left for school. "What should we do about this dentist bill—should we pay all of it, part of it, or none of it this month?" asked his wife. "I wish we didn't have dentist bills," he began. He was thinking back to his last pastorate, where the family dentist had given them professional courtesies. "But we do have this bill. If we pay it all this month, we cannot pay the department store," she said. "How shall we handle it?" "Boy, this family sure lives high on the hog," he complained. "We never seem to have anything left over to put aside for college. We just spend, spend, spend." "Wait a minute!" she burst in. "We are very careful about what we buy. I do not have a lot of the clothes I should have. You simply do not know how expensive it is just to live these days." "Now you listen to me," he countered, "I am a good provider for this family. When I took this church we thought we would be in clover, and now you're telling me I can't even pay all the bills this month. You must be doing something wrong!" They glowered at each other over the coffee cups and in that happy mood began their day in the service of the Lord.

The point of that scene is obviously that clergy do not have enough money to go around. The equally apparent solution is that if they were paid higher salaries they would not have such a problem. Of course you know that rampant inflation in the last decade has created what the economists call a money illusion. Even clergy are earning more money than they ever thought likely, but the cost of living countervails the income gains. So clergy think they should be paid more money to keep up with inflation. Although all of this is true and obvious, it is not my understanding of the problem.

Another apparent reason for advocating higher salaries is the sheer cost of family relationships. Poverty is not much of a Christian virtue unless it is linked to chastity! Like Abraham giving up Isaac to prove his faith, clergy families are expected to give way to the fact of limited financial resources. (I know a lot about that because I grew up in a

73

minister's family.) Ministers themselves may have very modest needs indeed and that is good and commendable. But their children go to school in the community and want to be part of that community and its activities. There are costs attached to such a lifestyle and one of the common ways of meeting the costs of family life is to have two incomes. An inordinately high number of clergy spouses are employed. On first thought one might say, "Good, if that's what they want to do." But once again the problem is seen in terms of the horizontal, personal dimension, and not in terms of vertical career patterns within a professional system. In the next chapter we will discuss the placement system, but note that one significant factor making placement difficult is the pattern of the working spouse. Two employment patterns are then involved in placement, not just one. (Solve one problem and you create another. That's how it is in systems.) So in this case, the apparent reason for advocating higher salaries is to sustain the family. Again, although true and obvious, that is not my understanding of the problem.

If money, as suggested in the opening paragraphs of this advocacy, gives us the power to make choices about our lives, then a relatively short supply of money will also affect the choices that clergy make. Here again the system is in conflict with itself. In the long process of required education of a high and humane quality, we whet the appetite for the finer things in life. Clergy enjoy books, theater, music, painting, et cetera, et cetera. But all those things come with price tags. In brief, a short supply of money circumscribes the choices you make about your own life-style and that of your family. The most common "ain't it awful" game that we play concerns the strain of putting our children through college. It is also a clear example of my point. Clergy greatly value higher education. They have known its delights and want the same for their families. But their resources conflict with their values. They sometimes feel stretched and very angry because they cannot live the way they think they ought to live. Again, although true and obvious, that is not my understanding of the problem.

A third leg in this true and obvious trilogy is professional status. At first glance this may seem the least powerful force, but it touches us most directly in our understanding of the problem. Clergy cannot help seeing themselves in relation to other people, especially in relation to other professional people. They know something of the fees associated with counseling, lectures, and managerial consultation. The clergy play all these roles, and yet they are not compensated anywhere near the normally expected levels. Even florists demand and receive high compensation for weddings and funerals. The clergy do not. Say what you will about the primacy of personal goals in terms of faithfulness, commitment, and sacrifice, still we are not existing on a remote island. We stand alongside others and we notice what they do, and as we notice others we measure ourselves by comparison. Clergy develop a subtle envy toward other professionals, not for their salaries but for their status. "They are doing so much better . . . I must be inept" is sometimes present in the darker recesses of the ministerial mind. True and obvious, and somewhat closer to the issue, but still not my understanding of the problem.

Understanding the Problem

The preceding tripartite explanation is one rationale for the reason clergy ought to have higher salaries. Most clergy have thought about these arguments many times. The common theme of all three is economic. Each in its own way defines the problem as economic and establishes a solution by economic means. There is no subtlety of symbolism in economics. But in attempting to define the problem correctly, subtle symbolism is required because ministerial salaries are, in truth, subtly symbolic.

In understanding the problem of clergy salaries, let us first correct a misnomer. Clergy are not salaried at all in the usual sense of that term. I have used the term without qualification as the culture does because clergy and other readers know what it means. But a more accurate appraisal begins with the perception that clergy are subsidized to be in a particular place. You need not do anything to receive this subsidy: just put in your time and be there. But of course that never happens in actual practice. The church and the professional systems expect activism. Do something: do it poorly or competently, but don't just sit there, do something. Such are the urgings of systems and their expectations will never disappear, but you can appreciate the kink they put in your perspectives on clergy compensation. Such a kink expresses itself in the tacit assumption that if you work harder and better you should receive a higher salary. Perspectives on compensation become even kinkier when we try to express ministerial compensation in terms of stewardship—but let me try.

The church system compensates you with the gift of time.

How you choose to use that time is a matter of stewardship. The church system also compensates you with the gift of location within a community. How you use that gift of location is a matter of stewardship. Part of the problem, then, is that parish clergy are far too comfortable with the cultural understanding of salary as payment for works done. Such an understanding avoids the harder questions of personal stewardship and accountability for the receipt of gifts.

Plans have been put forth for salary equalization of parish clergy, purporting to resolve the inequity of salary ranges within the profession. Such plans are both right and wrong. They are right when they understand salary as a subsidy for time; they are wrong in assuming no variance in community standards. Asking one to accept the gift of living in a particular community is also asking one to live as that community does, and if a minister does not want to live that way, he or she should decline the gift.

It is very difficult to be a steward of one's time and location—so difficult that most clergy do not even consider the question.

There are other facets of this complex problem, and understanding them requires even deeper probing. The last several generations of clergy have taken an enormous cut in pay. Not in inflated dollars, but in psychic pay. Even inflated dollars are still just inflated symbols, and it is to symbols that I am directing your attention. Everyone is living for psychic pay, dollars are merely symbols of the true compensation. When lay people receive a bonus (Latin for good) they are happy to have the money. But they are made content by the psychic symbolism. Given the hierarchies in this culture it is very hard for a boss to say to an employee, "You are a terrific worker, Harry. I love and approve of who you are and what you do." Instead of saying that, the boss hands the employee a bonus check, and the same communication takes place. Just let that exchange not happen and see how the employee feels about himself, his boss, and his work!

The cut in pay that clergy have taken is in the symbolic system. The Protestant church as we know and live with it today was formed in rural America, whose rural heritage still lives on in what we have been calling the church system. Pastors in nonaffluent, American frontier communities were much better stewards than their urbanized, affluent successors. They expected and received subsistence wages: a sack of potatoes, a house. (Yes, that is when the parsonage meant something special.) These things simply gave clergy time and a place to be. Their real pay was in community status. The most learned man in town, the arbiter of morals and ethics, the affirmer of justice and order, the educator, the healer: these were all part of the rural pastor's role and function, and he was paid for them in esteem.

Times have changed, and with them the pastor's status has been lowered, but the subsidy notion remains. The cut, then, to which I am directing your attention has to do with community status. The change is not necessarily bad. In urban culture we have more specialists and institutions to which more people have access. This is good, but it is different. As proof of their adaptability, clergy are in the process of changing from rural to urban models. That may be why the management of congregations has become popular in our day. Your predecessors could not have been what is known as pastoral directors. (Churches built on the frontier did not contain offices, they were not needed.) This is still a time of transition from rural to urban, the adaptation is still taking place, and rural vestiges live on. Today, the status of the clergy in a community has fallen, judged by rural standards. This is the psychic pay cut that clergy have taken, and it still hurts.

These understandings of the problem are essentially personal perceptions. They encourage you to understand the issues from the inside out, as it were. A fuller understanding requires you to stand outside and look around, for example, look at the way a system of low salaries produces unintended consequences. I invite you to get to know a system that produces incredible materialism among the clergy. Yes—the word is materialism! Clergy are very materialistic in the sense that they calculate the cost of every decision they make. I have a small habit that I will not let go of no matter how affluent I become, a habit which illustrates my materialism. Whenever I pick up a restaurant menu I inevitably read the price column first. Am I in a place I can afford? What particular entrée is in my price range? Finally, I check out what I would like to eat. That is materialism! It symbolizes what a system of low compensation does to the persons within it. Admittedly, this is not unique to the clergy. But we do have our unique manifestations of materialism, and what is worse we pretend that we do not.

In addition, the rampant individualism of the clergy, in their horizontal relationship with local churches, plays havoc with the vertical dimension of the profession in matters of compensation. Clergy rarely think about what their personal compensation means to the whole profession. One ministerial salary is set in comparison with another. When a majority of salaries are low, a system-wide pattern is set up. If a young minister with a family succeeds an older pastor with grown children who has not received a raise in twenty years, the young minister finds out how the system is a problem. The systemic problem of low salaries is seen not only in a one-to-one comparison but also in the larger recruitment patterns for the profession. Some young people who are well-qualified for ministry will opt for the choice of being active laymembers while earning a good living as, say, directors of laboratories. No one knows the long-range effect of the low salary factor on pastoral leadership—it could be formidable.

Having looked at the problem of low salaries, inside and out, I come now to my primary understanding of the problem. Clergy suffer from low self-esteem. That is why salaries are low. That is the reason they ought to be raised. Clergy think they are not worth very much. They are wrong. Unintentionally, the clergy have accepted without criticism the central economic value of this affluent culture, viz., one is worth what one produces. Athletes and movie stars make fortunes not because they deserve them but because stars produce greater income at the box office. Do you really think this is right? I do not. The worth of the clergy to the culture is simply not commensurate with their salaries, and in turn, clergy understand their low salaries to mean they are not worth much in this culture.

Nonsense.

Agenda Item 4: Salaries

Consider an Alternative

However correct the preceding explanation, not much will change as a result of my rhetoric. The most I can hope for is that you will think about the problem. I will rest my case for higher salaries where it is and keep pushing for it where I can. In the meantime, some modest interim steps may be considered.

Clergy have more economic power in their profession than they think they have and it should be exploited, in the best sense of the word. As individuals they do not have much power, but collectively they do.

Credit unions are a fine example of collective economic power. (This is not a how-to-do-it manual, you can find out how to do it if you want to do it.) They are owned by the members of an identifiable group. Basically, credit unions earn money for their shareholders and then loan money to them at lower than commercial interest rates. Credit unions are far more respectable in a self-respecting profession than the "take system" of professional discounts and courtesies.

Another interim suggestion that utilizes collective economic power is volume purchasing. In the luxury of rampant individualism, the clergy buys cars and projectors for personal and church use. Why not buy our common purchases in volume? We do not because we have not fully appreciated the vertical dimension in our profession. It is costing us millions. Can we afford to continue?

A Review of the Issues

Clergy compensation is not an economic issue. It is a personal and professional issue with economic implications.

The church and our professional system have conspired unwittingly to accept low salaries. The church system has only so many charitable dollars to spend, and our professional system has to take what is offered. The church and the clergy are in conflict, and both systems erode each other. But as a symbolic issue they must not be ignored. Morale and self-esteem may be intangible, but their presence have very tangible effects.

This advocacy has been one for economic change. Such change will be an effect, not a cause for esteem. Effecting change begins with a review of self-understanding and with a view of our profession as one of great worth, whether measured in terms of gifts, stewardship, or dollars.

Agenda Item 5:
Placement

BE IT RESOLVED: That there be greater peer participation in the placement system.

Background Notes on the Present System

Earlier, I gave you an unassailable piece of data: clergy move a lot. As the editor of an ecumenical journal for parish clergy, I know what a big job it is to keep track of their addresses. Another related piece of data is that parish clergy are not happy about the systems that facilitate their moves. This is harder to verify, but the absence of documentation does not undermine a widely held opinion, viz., no one likes a placement system which does not work in his or her interest.

To me, the widespread dissatisfaction with the placement system was a surprise. I knew there was grumbling in
free church polity—I had grumbled myself—but I had
always thought it was a problem unique to free church
polity. However, when I heard complaints from those
under appointment and from those in connectional
systems, I knew the problem was not just in free church
polity. There was something happening in all the systems.

Whatever its form, the placement system by its very
nature is a predictable crunch point. It is at the vortex of so
many church and professional systems that there is bound
to be a whirlpool, and many lives swirl around in its
function or dysfunction. For the laity, the issue is
competent leadership for their local church. For the
denomination, the issues are orderly procedure and the
supply of leadership. For the clergy, career patterns and
questions of success are at stake, not to mention personal
fulfillment and family security. With such a mix it is a
wonder that anything good happens at all.

The Person and the Process

Unsatisfied, Luke D. left the conference with his
denominational superior. He was disgruntled as he
climbed into his car for the ride back to First Church. He
was not disappointed in himself. He had mentally
rehearsed his remarks to Dr. Smyth, and they had been
communicated as he had hoped they would be both in style
and in content. He had been firm but not pushy, and
candid, but neither self-righteous nor self-deprecating. His
basic message had been clear: now was the time for him to
make a move. Now was right for him professionally, for the

congregation at First Church, and for the family. Yes, he had said all the right and necessary things.

It annoyed him that Dr. Smyth seemed bored with his story, and had acted as though he had heard it all before. Someday, Luke promised himself, if I ever get behind his desk I will not be bored when one of my ministers tells me something important! Sure, Dr. Smyth had said all the right things. He had commended him on the good reports he had heard about his ministry, and he had agreed that from Luke's point of view it might be time for a move. But it was what he did not say that disgruntled Luke. Dr. Smyth had not mentioned a single possibility for him to consider. In short, he was going home empty-handed. What was it Dr. Smyth had said when he brought up the vacancy at Sunnydale? Didn't Smyth say there were already dozens of requests for consideration at Sunnydale? How do those other guys hear about openings so fast? They must have nothing better to do than gossip about who is going where.

As he pulled up at First Church, Luke resolved that this *was* the time to move, and if Dr. Smyth would not be of much help he would have to figure out a way to get around him.

The story about Luke D. needs no denominational label. And Dr. Smyth could have been a bishop, a synod executive or a conference president. Parish clergy are often tempted to identify the bureaucracy with the incumbent, even when they are part of the bureaucratic machinery themselves. They are rather good at distancing *themselves* from the bureaucracy of the local church, and not very good at putting that same distance between denominational officials and systems. It is always easier to blame some one than some thing.

Dr. Smyth had reported that there were many potential candidates for a particular vacancy. Does that mean there is a clergy surplus? There is and there is not. The phrase surplus is a misnomer. More accurately, there is a clergy distribution problem. The unrelenting fact that impinges upon the placement system is that most Protestant churches are small. This varies from denomination to denomination, but as many as 75 percent of the churches may have less than two hundred members. In the jargon of the day, very small churches are not economically viable. Lyle Schaller has rightly pointed out that small churches are ideal for intimate fellowship. There is no shortage of openings in the smaller churches, but for clergy restless to move in their quest for success, the fewer number of larger churches are extremely selective in their pastoral search and there is much more competition. In sum, there are enough churches, but there is a surplus of clergy with expectations of upward mobility in proportion to the number of churches large enough to gratify their needs.

There is some experimentation underway with tent-making ministries. It is hoped that some of the smaller, economically marginal churches can be served by persons not requiring full-time compensation. It is a noble experiment and may prove of help in the distribution of clergy, but there are obstacles to overcome. The Bible points out that a man (or woman) cannot serve two masters. It is in the nature of work for responsibility to increase with ability. Churches may become the losers if part-time clergy increase their responsibility in part-time secular work.

Finally, it must be noted that the very terms placement and placement system need considerable qualification. Unexamined, the words connote a smooth uniformity in matching an equal number of persons with an equal number of positions. In fact, there are so many variables of persons and places that anything resembling uniformity is highly unlikely. In some denominations the placement system is not much more than a communication network; in others it is a guaranteed position (whether you like it or not). Let me warn parish clergy to be cautious of the assumptions they make about their placement systems and of the criticisms they make based on false assumptions.

Understanding the Problem

Whatever definition we give, whatever polity we follow, the common truth about placement systems is that they are asked to do more than they can deliver. My explanation may not cover new ground because you already know all the factors I am about to name, but I wonder if you have ever added them all up to understand why you grumble about placement.

The overload on the placement system begins with a professional anomaly. Parish clergy are expected to live in the community where the church is located. (In metropolitan areas the community may be a neighborhood.) To my knowledge very few vocations have this expectation about residency. Frankly, I never appreciated the power entailed in this aspect of the professional system until I worked on the magazine. My office was in downtown Chicago, and I could live where I wanted. It was a heady experience. Now that I am back in the pastorate I live two blocks from the church. No one said I had to do it that way, but if I lived twenty miles from the church there would be more than geographical distance between me and the congregation. So placement involves a community as well as a church.

A community is more than the name of a town. The community in which you live is where your children go to school. Defenders of the American educational system notwithstanding, there is great range of educational quality in this country. More than one minister has wanted to move to improve the children's educational opportunities.

A community also has sociological characteristics. Is it too snobbish to say that there are dull people in dull towns? We have already traced how learned professionals invest in years of schooling, cultivating their tastes and interests. Naturally, residency in a particular community circumscribes who your friends and associates will be. Sometimes, when ministers say they want to move because they need a challenge, they mean (forgive them—or understand them if you have been there) that the community is boring.

Further, the very work of ministry varies from community to community. In my first small-town pastorate I did far more counseling than I do now in a large suburban church. Why? Was I a better counselor then than now? Definitely not. I did more counseling there because there were fewer resources for doing what needed to be done. Community resources of all kinds vary. Some towns have great libraries, some do not. Some have adult education classes, some do not. Symphonies? Art leagues? American Associations of University Women? These are not nearly as far flung as the churches are. Some pastors create great ministries in developing such resources for their community, but others just miss what is lacking.

The point is that what began with one minister looking for a church has become one minister looking for a community in which to live, educate one's children, develop friends, and participate in community affairs. See how the burden on the placement system has grown?

And there is more weight to add. Another anomaly of the ministerial profession is housing. The call or appointment to a local church is associated with a parsonage, a manse, or a rectory. Need I elaborate on the variety of real estate in American Protestantism? It ranges from (near) lean-tos to mansions. Whatever its architectural style, no one manse can accommodate the many varieties of clergy families. Even the current trend toward housing allowances does not wholly solve the question of a manse. The house you love may not be the house you can afford, or it may be in a community you cannot afford to live in. (Admittedly, I am telling only the minister's side of the parsonage story. Trustees can tell you tales of what ministers have done to their manses.)

The placement system is now dealing with work, community, and housing. Only a penitentiary inmate has so much involved in location!

We now add another wrinkle, increasing the complexity even more, the working spouse. It may be due to the acceptance of women clergy, it may be due to our low salaries, it may be due to tent makers, it may be due to personal preferences, but whatever has done it this phenomenon is a new burden on the placement system.

Maybe what Luke D. was really saying to Dr. Smyth was, "Find me a church that matches my skills and interests, in a town full of cultural excitement, where my companions will be interesting, where my children will be well educated, where there's a four-bedroom house with low maintenance, and where there's a job for my wife as a professor of ornithology—and do it now."

There is simply no placement system, no placement officer, no placement opportunity that can meet so many expectations. But of course clergy are grumbling about the system: they have put their whole lives in its hands, and it cannot do the job.

Consider, for a moment, the other side of the equation. The local church and the denomination also have interests to be met in the placement system. In free church polity, and increasingly in connectional churches, lay leaders try very hard to define the needs of their congregation and the kinds of leadership that they believe will meet those needs. But sometimes their expectations are unrealistic for mere humans. As one wag put it, "This church wants a minister who will walk on the water—and not splash!" These high expectations should be taken as a flattering compliment and not as a job description. A problem for the laity to which clergy should be more sensitive is the necessity of making important decisions about clergy on smidgens of specific information. Some clergy have become very good candidates at the expense of learning to be very good ministers.

The focus of clergy disgruntlement about the placement system is the denomination's machinery and officials. Is this justified? Sometimes—incompetence is no respecter of titles. For the most part, however, the complicating factor is higher clergy expectations, not bureaucratic failures. All hierarchies have inequities, and the denominational system cannot be expected to provide even-handed order over the whole process.

The primary focus in both the denominational and the lay systems is ministerial performance in the particular context of a local church. Clergy should remember that all the other issues concern their professional agenda and that they precipitate from the anomalies of their unique system of work and life.

Consider an Alternative

For the clergy the best alternative is to better understand what they are trying to accomplish. I believe that this new understanding will require more ambition than a system matching persons to positions can deliver. But it is not necessarily the fault of the system that complications abound.

Going back to the keynote remarks preceding these advocacies, I claimed that the denominational church exerts considerable influence over the clergy because of a vacuum at the center caused by clergy not taking responsibility for their own profession. Recognizing that dynamic, I am advocating greater peer participation in placement. I do realize that certain polities seem to require tighter denominational control than I am recommending, but surely an intermediate, even advisory, step, would be useful.

Specifically, because so much is at stake in placement, it would be better to disperse some of the responsibility for the placement system. Instead of meeting with Dr. Smyth and declaring his need to move, it might have helped Luke D. to first have a conference with his peers. At such a conference they could help him better understand his own motives. (If you have followed all the advocacies closely it is apparent that a minister would probably want to share the smaller professional goals he has established for success.) Peer involvement could help the laity on a search committee know the candidates better as well as help prospective pastors know more about a particular church. In addition, those peers who take turns on the review committees would certainly understand more about the complications of placement, so that when their time came to think about a new pastorate they would understand how complicated the process has become.

This advocacy may most help the beleaguered denominational official, who must groan and grumble under the weight of the placement process. It is sound biblical insight and good management theory that a heavy burden of decision is lightened by being shared.

A Review of the Issues

Placement is the necessary consequence of an institutionalized church. Here, personal freedom of choice and the maintenance of order are clearly in conflict. So many systems are interconnected in placement that it is hard to know which string will untangle the knot. In this advocacy, I prefer to place the initiative for change with the ministerial profession. The need to move and the related advocacies on success and salary are clearly related to the tangle of placement. If that urgency were diminished through redefinition of success and improved financial conditions, much of the pressure on the placement system would be diminished, and the whole church could do a better job of dealing with our broadened expectations.

My central thesis seems even more helpful as the tangle of placement unfolds: if we would assume greater responsibility for our own profession, the whole church—as well as the clergy—would be liberated for the pursuit of its mission.

Agenda Item 6:
Use of Time

BE IT RESOLVED: That clergy work less and have more fun.

Background Notes on the Present System

It is not a contradiction in terms to say that I want to be serious about having fun. When I say this to an audience of clergy I can count on a titter of laughter in the room. They think (or hope) I have put this one on the agenda as a comic relief after some heavy going. Clergy are wrong about my intentions, but right about the need for relief.

In the advocacy about ministerial salaries it was stated that one of the gifts given to the profession is that of time. It is an important and serious gift. When you feel discouraged about your vocation it helps to be reminded that no other profession is so lavish and generous in the amount of time it bestows upon its practitioners.

The subject of time management has recently attracted attention. Speed Leas and others have written some very practical books on how to better manage your time. I will not retrace that ground, but invite you to think in terms of personal freedom and collective options for the use of time. In this analysis these are the twin foci. Parish clergy have problems with the use of time because their personal independence offers them an inordinately high degree of freedom to shape their own lives and work. Further, because of our culture's excessive emphasis on individualism, they rarely think of utilizing time in collective ways with their peers.

Personal freedom and collective options for the use of time are serious subjects, even when applied to having fun.

The Person and the Process

John H. was attending a workshop for parish clergy on time management. Using Gestalt psychology with good experiential methodology, the leader invited participants to take out their pocket calendars—those tyrannical little books that tell us what we should do and when we should do it. The exercise involved talking out loud to one's datebook, telling it your feelings in regard to its demands upon you. In an uncharacteristically demonstrative act, John H. took his little black book and flung it against the nearest wall. At first, the other participants were astonished, then they laughed, and finally joined in the act of protest. Presumably it was therapeutic for all.

Agenda Item 6: Use of Time

Later, in analyzing the meaning of his act, John said he was simply overcome with rage. While thumbing the pages he had seen weddings slated months in advance, committee meetings scheduled through eternity, and notations of anniversary calls he should make on particular days. It seemed to him as if his whole life were plotted out for him, that he was living his life to the beat of the calendar's drums, but he knew its cadence was not what he wanted to march to.

The others concurred in feeling controlled by the book, but countered that it was a necessary evil, a way of bringing some order out of chaos. They were saying that planning ahead was a way of maximizing their effectiveness. In specific contexts, John H. admitted the truth of these remarks, but was unrelenting in his rage at the total impact the datebook had upon him.

Clergy have few status symbols. Persons who are drowning in the accouterments of the good life have clothes, cars, and addresses appropriate to their status. There is not much prestige for clergy in all those things. The crowded calendar is the ministerial equivalent of clothes, cars, and addresses. It says (or we think it says) to the laity and to our peers, "I must be all right—see how much in demand I am." The datebook is a helpful device when clergy want to play the "ain't it awful" game. Ain't it awful how hard I work. Ain't it awful how little time I spend with my family. Ain't it awful how little time I have for. . . . Clergy are good at this game; to them it means: So much to do, and so little time in which to do it. Surely the kingdom of God would come to this place if only I had more time.

Baloney!

The phenomenon of the crowded datebook with its meaning as a game and its power over professional patterns is what theologians call works righteousness. In brief, this phrase means that we are saved not by who we are or who God is, but by what we do. We shall *work* our way into the kingdom of heaven. Never mind that such a notion is unsound biblically and theologically, and although clergy may preach this truth, they do not apply it to their lives and profession.

I suggest that the datebook has emerged as a powerful symbol because of the vacuum in the profession about personal and professional identity. Chances are that your datebook is crowded with the agenda of others. You respond more than you initiate. Church systems superimpose time frames and work functions on your own identity patterns. John H. throws his datebook at the wall because he is angry about the absence of reciprocity, angry at himself for not being an equal partner in shaping his time and task responsibilities.

Thus another puzzling dilemma emerges. On the one hand, included in the profession is the gift of time and an inordinately high degree of freedom in managing and accounting for that gift. On the other hand, clergy feel tyrannized and frustrated by the many claims upon their time and by the loss of personal and professional freedom that such claims affect. In the struggle with this dilemma there are winners and losers. In the present system the winners are the laity, the denomination, and the functions of the pastor. (Incidentally, it seems clear to me that the winners are short-term winners but long-term losers.) The losers are the pastor's family, the profession, and the pastor as a person. In a profession with so much freedom it seems fatuous to call for liberation of the clergy, but we need to be liberated from some powerful, self-inflicted forces that make us work addicts.

Understanding the Problem

Speaking in an interview for *The Christian Ministry,* Howard Clinebell of the School of Theology in Claremont, California, said, "Clergy tend to have a high work addiction, and a high pleasure anxiety." This is a statement about the ministerial personality. It may differ in degree for each of us, but as a professional trait it is generally descriptive. Why is that?

The insights of transactional analysis have helped us to understand that our personalities have several dimensions. In TA terms, clergy live their professional lives in the "Parent" dimension of their personality. Like it or not we symbolize religious authority to the congregation. We may disavow such a label, but we probably utilize its power in relation to individuals and the congregation. We are work addicts because that makes us feel very responsible. We are responsible to God and man, to the congregation and to the individuals in it. But responsible in what way? That is the issue. A lot of clergy liberation begins when clergy move out of their Parent selves and into their "Adult" selves.

Here we have a practical conceptualization tool that shifts our focus from Parent to Adult and gives a liberating dimension to responsibility. If you conceptualize your relationship to a congregation, saying, "My obligation to this church is not to do its ministry, but to see to it that ministry takes place within it." This is a profound differentiation between responsibility and role and function.

Two contemporary movements have coalesced giving form and substance to such a conception. They are the small group movement and management by objectives. This is not the place to delve into the merits of these two experiential and conceptual movements, but for those who have tasted their power a new liberation becomes possible. Clergy need not even attend every meeting in the church, or call upon every member of the congregation, or be in their offices seven days a week. The groups in each church are working, and the plan is to involve the groups in charting their own goals. It is that process and not the person who directs it that frees the clergy from superimposed roles and functions.

So far, we have tried to understand the problem as one of self-conceptualization. That is only half of the problem. The other half is external to the minister as a person, but nevertheless intrudes in ways that must be acknowledged. The practice of parish ministry poses an anomaly, a different pattern from the ordinary. The placement system is complicated by the anomaly of requiring you to live in the community where you work. Similarly, the management of your time is affected by the anomaly that you are working within a voluntary organization. By cultural standards this sets the clergy in an atypical pattern. In short, clergy work most when others are at leisure.

The times of our greatest involvement with a local church are weekends, evenings, and holidays. The Ten Commandments dictate that we keep the sabbath day holy, and that we do. They also dictate that we not work on the sabbath; that we do. The lay congregation does not work on the sabbath, but we do. This is an anomaly. Except in specialized retirement communities all church boards and committees meet at night, a time when the lay congregation is free of its secular duties and free to meet as the church. In short, for lay people church meetings are leisure-time activities; for the clergy the meetings are work. My children look forward to the holiday seasons because they break the routine of school days. But I do not look forward to the holidays in the same way that they do. At that time my routine is heavier, and my Child self wants to get out from under the church duties and enjoy the holidays like my children—as well as with my children. I am in the middle of an anomaly.

The anomaly of the voluntary organization being open for business during its constituency's leisure time is hard on the clergy, but we make it more difficult by then adding to our peculiar pattern the normal cultural work week. So there you have the full, complicated picture. Clergy have the worst of both worlds: normal secular work patterns plus special work patterns during others' leisure times. This is confining.

The problem, then, is a work-addicted personality wed to the anomaly of a peculiar working pattern. If that is a happy marriage, why do we revere and despise our datebooks?

Consider an Alternative

Congregations are more pliable than the clergy. (And more pliable than clergy expect them to be.) Members lready think you are busy, but are quite vague on just what ait is that you do. See how pliable they are—they just hold the views you have taught them! Suppose you were to teach them another view. Would they understand it and accept it? My experience has been that they will, but you must initiate the teaching. If you do not, you had better follow the patterns they are accustomed to.

First, I invite you to consider working a five-day week. The American labor movement reached this goal in 1935. The clergy are not even close to that goal. Clergy talk about a day off with great unction, as if their claim were honored more in breach than in practice. Stay away from the church two days a week, you will be better for it, and so will the church. Do not do this without first teaching the congregation what this means and why you do it. They will be fascinated about the business of weekends, nights, and holidays. Perhaps they have never heard that said before.

Clergy should teach their congregations how to use ministerial services. Laity do what they do because no one has ever taught them differently. For instance, the congregation goes to the trouble and expense to provide the minister with an office, a telephone, and maybe a secretary. But the whole provision is circumvented when a parishioner calls you at home at night to talk about church business. If the congregation wants to do it that way, they could have saved a lot of money! That is not the way they want to do it, of course, but unless you teach them to call you at the church, where your files are, unless you teach them not to tell your spouse or children what they want you to know, unless you teach them to call for an appointment, as they do their dentist, they will not know that this is how a minister should be used. The ball is in your court. If you do not choose to teach them how to use you, then make your peace with how they do so.

The second part of this advocacy is that clergy should have more fun. I enjoy the camaraderie of my peers; some of my best friends are clergy. I enjoy it because we meet in our Adult selves, not as Parents, and not as Children. I have already implied that a lot of denominational meetings are really ruses to get together with one's colleagues. (Properly entering the meeting in your datebook even makes its fun aspects legitimate.) If what I am implying is foreign to your experience of denominational church gatherings, next time you go force yourself out of the assembly and see what is happening in the adjoining halls and coffee shops. You will be amazed to see clergy at play!

If my hunch is right that clergy enjoy one another's company, consider building the collective power of your profession from there. Why not charter a bus for your colleagues and spouses to go to the theater or concert? Doing something like that not only has potential economic benefits, it also diminishes the barriers of individualism that are manifest even in our leisure activities.

The denomination errs in not sponsoring the equivalent of the company picnic. At regular intervals the judicatories should host a golf outing, a tour, or a dinner party at their expense. Even the military has programs of rest and relaxation. Are clergy immune from the need for R and R? It may sound extravagant for the denomination to squander its limited resources on such foolishness, but the investment is based on self-interest. The denominational church needs the trust and ownership of the churches and clergy in its constituency. The dividend of such gatherings would be the rapport that builds when colleagues meet as Adults.

A Review of the Issues

The subject of this advocacy has been time, time used to work and to play. However, time has not been the central issue. The real issue has not been named, but its presence is implicit: the issue is trust. Clergy work too much not because there is too much to do, but because they do not trust that the process will work and the work will be done. Clergy play too little because they do not trust the recuperative process of their own spirits. The work they do is not taxing physically, but it is draining emotionally and spiritually. Although the drain is not likely to appear at church, it is likely to appear at home. The advocacy about work and play could have a major benefit for the relaxation of tension in the parsonage.

Finally, this advocacy may seem to have veered away from my central thesis, that clergy should be responsible for their profession. It has not at all. This is an enabling advocacy. If clergy have work addictions and pleasure anxieties, it is because they do not trust that the work of the church can be done by clergy and laity. They will continue to work hard and play little until they have a healthier sense of self, until experience confirms that they are part of a support system and are following processes that are trustworthy. Through work and play come trust, and through trust liberation.

Agenda Item 7:
Selectivity for
Older Ministers

BE IT RESOLVED: That retirement be a time of maximum freedom for retired ministers.

Background Notes on the Present System

In some ways this advocacy should have been first, because it is the summation toward which the other advocacies are moving. It is placed last, not on a scale of priorities, but in line with the vertical career pattern. Retirement is the flowering of that which has taken root long before.

Alas, this does not happen in the present system. If it is a scandal that young practitioners are dumped into inappropriate first parishes and left to their own strivings without help from their peers, the treatment of older persons in the profession is a scandal of greater power, scope, and sadness. Young ministers can recover and correct the mistakes of the present system; older ministers must live with them.

The whole American citizenry is growing older. We live longer. Clergy, in fact, have a longer life expectancy than those in most other vocations. And under the present system they also have less to do in retirement. This advocacy presupposes that professional life and activity are not limited to forty years, but only by the way the profession plans for and encourages ministers to make choices for themselves.

It is hard to express in numerical dates the time of life that is included in this advocacy. Certainly sixty-five is not a God-given number. (It came from Bismarck's Germany over a hundred years ago.) The Social Security system and the pension plans of the denominations urge us to consider retirement in terms of this age. I prefer to conceive of retirement as a time of an individual's consolidation of interests, a time of lessened financial responsibilities and greater choices about one's life, location, and contribution.

Hopefully, we can design a system which in the future will offer a good selection of choices. Unhappily, the present system does not offer such choices.

The Person and the Process

Abraham B. pruned his rose garden. Garden? Do three shrubs on a balcony make a garden? Every day he pruned the roses, whether they needed it or not. He was dressed in a shirt and tie—not exactly gardening attire, but when you get up in the morning and dress in a shirt and tie for forty years it is hard to change. He and Sarah were comfortable at Leisure Towers. They had all their creature needs met, even if in somewhat cramped conditions. Abraham had come to Leisure Towers with a certain satisfaction. After all, he had led his congregation to make a pledge when the denomination had proposed to refurbish the old Stratford Tower Hotel. Of course, he and Sarah would have liked to stay on in the last community, but the church needed the parsonage for a new minister. "Fine young man," Abraham said of him, although he did not really know him. The real estate market had gone sky high so that buying a home there was out of the question. The hardest part of the move to Leisure Towers had been parting with their household belongings, especially his books. He had written to his seminary, but they said they could not shelve all the books they already had. No one seemed to want them. There are not many bookshelves in a two-room apartment, so his books ended up at the rummage sale.

Some of the things he and his wife had thought they were going to do they had not done. Abraham wanted to do some of the writing he had put off during the "active" ministry—that's what he always called those forty years of his life, but he never called these years "the inactive ministry." He had been given an interim pastorate in Florida, but a tragedy struck in December: they called a minister. "Fine young man," Abraham said. They had traveled some, but Sarah's health was not all that good and, well, it just became too expensive to keep on the go.

Snip, snip, snip went the pruning scissors. "We have a letter from Corrie Whitterspoon," Sarah announced, coming out on the porch into the warm morning sun. "She says the church is in an uproar over the plan to sell the vacant lot next to the church." "Are they?" said Abraham, thinking to himself, "I could have told you that. They were in an uproar about it seven years ago." Snip. Snip.

They kept pretty busy in their retirement living. They went to church every Sunday. There were activities in the Towers—cards, games, and that sort of thing—and the town offered quite a few programs for senior citizens. They especially enjoyed the concerts in the park. And he still knew some of the other clergy who lived in the Tower. They got together regularly, but mostly they just talked about old friends they knew or had known.

Snip—he cut off one of the tender blossoms. Was it by mistake or on purpose?

One must be careful about advocacies concerning older people. There is a great temptation to become romantic about older people, and another to tell them what to do. Both temptations are to be resisted. Cantankerous, incompetent young people just become cantankerous, incompetent old people; there is no guarantee of mellowing with age. Further, *not* telling older people what they ought to do is the very advocacy that I will make here. So, no romance and no orders.

Before citing the elements of scandal in the treatment of older ministers, one must acknowledge some areas of great progress. Most denominations have pension programs. That is progress. Unfortunately, they are keyed to salaries, so many older ministers still receive small pensions. Further, the inclusion of clergy under Social Security and

Agenda Item 7: Selectivity for Older Ministers

Medicare has been beneficial to many recent retirees. Another plus is a cultural awakening to the presence of older people in general which has helped the ministerial profession in particular. Some of the Gray Panthers used to wear clerical collars. Also on the plus side, the current generation of practicing ministers is more aware of retirement planning. Whether they do this or not, they are at least aware that the present is the time to plan for the future.

Part of the consciousness-raising that has been happening recently is an increased awareness that retirement is not a static stage in life, but one that passes through many stages. To name just a few, early retirement has a foot-loose and fancy-free dimension, when one may travel or become engrossed in deferred pleasures. Later, retirees reach a settled-in stage when they want stability and deeper roots, often in a community of kindred souls. Then there is a stage of relinquishment, when one gives up the car and some of the self-care habits of a lifetime. Whatever names are used to describe these stages, one unassailable fact emerges: retirement planning that does not allow for changes within this period is disastrous.

Professor Bernice Neugarten of the University of Chicago is a social scientist specializing in gerontology. With people living longer and longer, she recognized the need to restructure "old" into several differentiated classes, and so coined the much-publicized term, "the young-old." She insists that the young-old are the fastest growing group in America. They have considerable energy and vitality, but little opportunity for utilizing life's experiences. Although I cannot apply the truth of that observation to the whole of society, it certainly applies to the clergy and will continue to apply as that group grows in size, unless the present system is changed.

In truth, there is not much of a retirement system at all. When most clergy leave their last church they enter a new and unknown world. Even though there are deficiencies in the church and in the ministry, both the church and the profession have given the clergy some sense of identity. The problems that emerge when clergy disengage from parish ministry are proof of the power their professional role has had in shaping their identity. When newly retired clergy find themselves sitting in the pews with their spouses they wonder who they are.

They are ministers without churches. The power of the horizontal church relationship is evident in retirement. In other words, when you break the horizontal relationship, you find out just how strong that tie really is and how weak the professional tie is. Many retired clergy suffer from a loss of self-esteem. Their worth as persons had been affirmed by the supportive community of a local church, and when that is gone they feel inadequate.

It is in that loss that the profession has a responsibility. Retired clergy should still be part of a supportive community—the whole profession.

This advocacy is a plea that we offer options to older ministers. The present system proscribes who they are, what they do, and how they live. But if clergy want to disengage from church relationships, let them do so. If clergy want to depart from the profession, let them do so. If they want to follow a second career, let them do so. But let *them* select the path they want to follow. If they want to remain as part of churches and part of the profession, then let them choose that option. But we had better have a system for letting them do so.

Understanding the Problem

The problem is that retired clergy have few options. The professional system does not offer them choices. Clergy do what they can, not what they want.

While a pension plan as opposed to no plan is a step forward, rewards and arbitrary rules pose major problems. The administrators of pension plans are quick to point out what cannot be done. It is our responsibility to let them know what ought to be done.

Let us begin with the first problem we face in retirement: Where shall we live? The parsonage system may have been beneficial during forty years of work in local churches, but when that work ends so does the housing. For years soaring real estate costs have exceeded even the resources of the prudent, and when one has no equity in a house, housing costs upon retirement are awful. Pension funds could help solve this problem in one of two ways. (Before continuing, I must acknowledge that different denominations have different means of funding and computing pensions. This means that each denomination will have to figure out how to meet these ends in its own way.)

Upon retirement clergy should have the option of a portion of their retirement fund being available for downpayment on a house. This would obviously reduce the principal, and the subsequent pension would be smaller, but it would help the minister make a choice about home ownership, an option that is currently denied him. Pension funds are held in trust and invested for return, so why not invest these funds in low-interest mortgages for clergy who want to buy homes? How can the investment suffer if the houses revert to the denominations in the event of default? Meantime, clergy have some choices concerning their housing. Or, to take the concept a step further, why not have clergy form not-for-profit corporations to build, own, and manage retirement housing for them which they could finance by long-term, low-interest loans from their pension funds? The "prudent man" concept in law applies to investment policies for trust funds, but surely it is prudent to invest in housing for retired clergy when there is protection on the principal.

Second, at a specific age certain forces come into play that tell a minister what to do. These forces may be mandatory retirement rules, eligibility for Social Security, and the beginning of pension payments. Whose interests are met by these rules? Not necessarily those of the clergy. Let the clergy have a range of options about the age of retirement and what they will do in retirement.

Consider the following possibility as what could happen if clergy are given some selectivity. A minister turns sixty, is in good health, and still loves his work. His children are grown, and his financial obligations have been reduced. He is the pastor of a large church. Instead of waiting until age sixty-five, let him draw on his pension early, but in smaller amounts. Next, if the denominational systems were enlightened, they could urge this pastor to seek placement in one of those economically marginal churches whose number is plentiful. They might even subsidize such an arrangement. Thus, between small salary, small pension, and small subsidy, an economically marginal church has a full-time, competent and experienced leader. The minister does not have the many responsibilities of a larger church, he has not lost his involvement with the local church, and he has left a vacancy for someone else to fill. I cannot say how many takers there would be because the option is not currently available.

If you have read my analysis in sequence, you will notice that this advocacy relates to placement. The alleged clergy surplus, or deployment crunch, could be redistributed if some of the clergy took early retirement and accepted smaller pastorates. Even without their acceptance of a pastorate you would still be affecting the redistribution of clergy to the smaller churches. So let the ministers take early retirement and go on to teaching, writing, or basketweaving—or whatever they want to do next. A system that rigidly keeps them locked in pastorates until some magic age also keeps the system inequitably distributed.

Pension systems are not the only rigidities that clergy face. When one moves from pastorate to pastorate the moving expenses are borne by the church to which one is moving. But who pays for the move from the last church to retirement? Clergy pay it themselves. What a terrific farewell gift from the system! You work forty years and they shake your hand and give you a moving bill. Is this life in a humane, people-centered institution? Should not each denominational judicatory have a kitty that pays for the last move? It would be a modest enough gift of appreciation.

Health insurance is now available in the pastorate. When a minister retires in some denominations he loses group coverage. This is also sad. Some caring agency should also see that health insurance is kept in force for retired clergy.

The whole problem of limited choices in retirement goes back to that horizontal/vertical tension. So much is geared to one's role in the pastorate, but so little thought is given to the lifelong pilgrimage of that person. The laity and the denominational church have some responsibility here, but far and away the responsibility rests with the professionals, who should know more clearly than anyone that if you pursue the ministry from ordination to death there are special, predictable needs in the vertical span. Anticipating this, the profession should move to have those needs met.

Consider an Alternative

No one takes away your robe and Bible when you retire. Unintentionally, however, your professional status is taken. An alternative is to keep retired clergy close to the profession. Not so close as to invite meddling, but close enough to invite inclusion. Denominational bodies should have advisers. When there are meetings planned, why not have the retired clergy meet first to review plans and purposes? They have been to hundreds of meetings. They can tell a denominational executive what to expect and what to avoid. Every judicatory has a pool of experience and talent that it is not using.

In the first advocacy we spoke of the initiation of the young. There is a strange affinity between the young and the old: neither has much to lose or to prove. Perhaps those professional tutors that I mentioned earlier could be gray-haired. Local churches have never known what to do with the title emeritus. I have a suggestion: adopt a retired minister and name him or her the emeritus minister of a beginner-pastorate. Stay in close touch; the beginniner, the experienced professional, and the local church will be better for it.

Now for the present incumbents in the profession, never take counsel together without the retired ministers. They know something you don't—what lies ahead on the vertical dimension. Their very presence will remind you that today's patterns shape tomorrow.

Retirement is a professional issue, not just individually, but collectively in terms of policies and their consequences. Ordination admits you into the practice of a profession. Retirement should not automatically dismiss you.

A Workshop on Professional Associations

This preliminary workshop now begins the process of response to the keynote and seven advocacies. It will survey what is available, suggest a structure appropriate for sustained growth, and offer a report from one fledgling professional association for clergy.

The Means of Change

The first stage in affecting change is an individual's perception of need, and individual action through infiltration. However, if this were the only option available for changing the system the impact would be modest, perhaps just a slight change in attitude. But the process of change usually begins slowly.

Now, when you attend an ordination, you will muse over the possible ordination process that could take place as the ordinand begins parish ministry. Maybe when you feel the urge to make a pastoral change, you will sit down to define what you mean by success. Maybe when you are bored by a continuing education experience, you will ask, who does this benefit? Maybe when you hear a colleague bemoan the raw deal he or she has had from the denomination when requesting a pastoral change, you will wonder which of the multiple factors in placement were unsuccessfully resolved. Maybe when you glance at your datebook it will whisper to you of work addictions and pleasure anxieties. And maybe when you meet an older minister you will have a glimpse of your future which is presently forming.

All of these involve changes in perceptions. You might say your consciousness has been "raised." However, you really have been conscious of these problems all the time, they are the daily stuff of professional life. What has been raised is the validity of your own data. Just keep on looking and wondering about what affects clergy and why clergy allow certain things to take place.

Infiltration means that as an individual parish minister relating to a local congregation, denomination, or ministerium, you can begin to teach, interpret—yes, even advocate—the meaning of the data you have gathered on the profession. At all its levels, in the day-to-day deliberations of the church you can effect a slight change. But the most likely changes of any significance will be in yours and others' individual internal perceptions of what it means to be a professional.

The second stage for effecting change is the denomination, where you meet with colleagues. One may wish that we were not divided into denominations, but we are, and we have to start from there. I am very conscious of the presence and power of the denominational church, and throughout these advocacies have maintained the thought—subject to differing polities—in the front of my mind. Having presented these advocacies to clergy of almost every denominational polity, I can predict many of your responses, and I know they will not be uniform. But I believe that first clergy will need to meet and work together in their denominational context before broader professional change can be accomplished. Nevertheless, I do not believe that involvement by professionals within denominational structures will affect change for the entire church system because in changing a denomination's professionals one still has not changed the professional system itself. These advocacies are based on wider ambitions, although they will need to begin with an agenda that is best suited to a particular denominational ethos.

In recent years there have been several attempts to organize clergy across denominational lines. In the late 1960s there were sporadic attempts at unionization. I have always resisted unions for clergy, as they are contrary to my mind-set. A union implicitly assumes that "what ails us is them, if we can get us together we can deal with them," whereas I think what ails us is us. We need to get us straightened out. Furthermore, the Christian church neither needs nor deserves enmity between the laity and the clergy. We are both part of the church and must function within it, despite differing self-interest.

There are already professional agencies available to

begin the implementation of these advocacies in limited ways. Consider what is available. If the advocacy on continuing education seems of highest priority, you should know of the Academy of Parish Clergy and the Society for the Advancement of Continuing Education for Ministry (SACEM). Both organizations came into being in the 1960s and both work to raise standards in continuing education. Neither is as chauvinistic as the advocacy in this book, which cites clergy initiative in procuring what is needed as the missing factor in continuing education. The Academy of Parish Clergy is modeled after the Academy of General Practice of the medical profession. Membership requires certification of so many hours in advanced studies. SACEM is an amalgamation of seminary and institute offerings specializing in studies for the parish ministry. In addition to these two there are various independent and seminary-related institutes and specialized agencies for continuing education. None of these are wide ranging professional organizations.

Finally, almost every community has an organization of clergy. These are known as ministerial associations, councils of churches, or simply clergy fellowships. They differ widely in purpose and program. Almost always they are local and functional—"Who will host the Good Friday service this year?" Rarely do they deal with substantive professional issues.

It would be a very rewarding experience for such a local ministerium to share this book as a year-long study project. Where I have alluded to denominational differences, pastors of other denominations could fill in the specific data. Such a discussion would facilitate professional rapport and could be the beginning of a more intentional professional organization.

Thus, there are already numerous structures where clergy meet together as professionals. All of these could become effective vehicles for change if their intentions were shifted to the task of filling the vacuum at the center of the profession. But even if the existing organizations are used, it is helpful to have a model toward which to work so I am offering the material that follows. My model is clearly fictional, as it does not presently exist. It is also experimental, because until we learn by doing, we will not have the feedback which will enable us to correct mistakes in design. But it helps to have a plan for comparative purposes. It also helps to have some proposal as a sounding board in responding to these advocacies.

The Shape and Style of a Professional Association

We begin to sketch organizational form by outlining its style and shape. The unswerving principle of design is that an organization must be appropriate to the nature of its profession. The American Medical Association is appropriate to a profession of individual entrepreneurs. It is not appropriate to a profession like ours.

For one thing, a professional association of clergy must be intentionally Christian. The reason is both simple and profound. The simple reason is that clergy are committed to the Christian life, and it would be worse than foolish to park our Christianity outside the door. More profoundly, within the Christian tradition there is a process essential to our organization. Theologians try to explain this process through words like grace, covenant, freedom, and others

121

from the theological lexicon. But even they admit the futility of their task. Finite words cannot express the full range of the Christian community's capacity for renewal, reform, and creativity. The Christian church has existed for so long because it has a capacity to renew and reform and recreate itself as an institution. It is this quickening process that will be required in a professional association of clergy.

Second, a professional association of clergy must be voluntary. The need for voluntarism is not so much to maximize individual freedom in a collective structure as it is to allow individuals to own that structure. The word voluntary comes from the Latin verb, *volo,* meaning I will. Our choice is one of participation and support. The voluntary nature of such a professional organization will keep it responsive to the needs of participants. And being voluntary it will also be a check against triumphant clericalism.

Third, a professional association of clergy would be limited to practicing professionals. This is an exclusive principle. It is also chauvinistic, eliminating clergy who are not parish ministers, as well as laity and students. While the full organizational plan will include liaison with those special groups, they would not be included in the association of clergy because they already have their own organizations. Drawing on the framework of transactional analysis, a professional association needs to be exclusive to enable the Adult-to-Adult meeting of collegial groups.

Fourth, a professional association of clergy would be interdenominational. There may be denominational caucus groups, but the organization must be open to all denominational traditions that choose to participate. The

122

crucial factor here is whether or not the agenda is appropriate to all denominations. I think it is, but an agenda cannot be a reality until it is developed and owned by its constituents who have come to consensus.

A professional association of clergy will be local at first and the local groups federated with one another where necessary. The common denominator for clergy is their current context of ministry. A Presbyterian pastor in Atlanta, Georgia, does not have as much in common with a Presbyterian pastor in Boise, Idaho, as he does with the Methodist, Episcopal, and Southern Baptist clergy of Atlanta. The local context of ministry takes precedence over denominational labels.

Fifth, professional association must be covenantal. Expectations regarding member participation must be declared and the agenda defined. Groucho Marx uttered an important truth in a wacky way when he said, "I wouldn't belong to any organization that would have me as a member." Applied in the context of covenant this truth means that the organization must set high standards of performance and participation and exclude those who do not wish to meet them.

Specifically, a professional association of clergy should cost the participants money and time. Hardly any of the current clergy organizations ask much from their participants. This one should. Membership fees should be high in order to accomplish the many programs it would sponsor, and because where one's treasure is there also rests one's heart. A commitment of time is absolutely necessary. Nothing good happens in a voluntary organization unless one's time is invested lavishly. This will be a working organization, and the work will take time. If one does not wish to put up the time and the money one ought not participate, for without these it will fail. The covenant has rigorous terms, and this may dissuade people from participating, but it must have them to succeed because expectations are high. What follows is a design that embodies these expectations.

The Function of a Professional Association

The functions of a professional association will become clearer through the following hypothetical organization. I hope this creation will help you to formulate other ideas rather than limit your conceptions.

The Professional Association of Parish Clergy in Galilee County, Illinois, has ninety-seven members from twenty-three different denominations. The covenant is twenty hours of active participation from each member per month. The annual membership fee is based on a sliding scale, but the average is two hundred dollars, giving the association a budget of about twenty thousand dollars. They meet once a month in plenary session, and many times in smaller groups.

Annually, each member writes his or her personal growth goals. This plan includes personal growth, professional growth, pastoral objectives, and educational needs. Each plan is reviewed by one's peers—sometimes the local congregation is consulted, sometimes the denominational church. After the plan has been reviewed, each member contracts with the association for the year. He or she may wish assignment to a particular work group, request certain education, or propose a venture that is new to him- or herself and to the organization. Each member is reviewed by colleagues at the end of the year to evaluate how goals have been met.

There are seven standing committees in the association, which serve as program bodies. Each member must participate on one of the committees. Not surprisingly, they are orientation to the parish, career development, continuing education, finance, placement, recreation, and retirement. There are also subcommittees, such as the credit union of the finance committee. The continuing education committee is especially busy because it purchases the educational services the clergy have requested.

In addition to the standing committees the association has special fellowship groups. These include nonparish clergy, such as students and retired ministers. There are also denominational caucuses.

Direction for the organization is provided by a dean elected every two years and a board of managers representing each of the seven standing committees, as well as five members elected at large. The decision-making authority is vested in the constituents, who express themselves at the monthly plenary meetings.

In retrospect, the members take great pride in what they have accomplished within the past year. There are six beginning pastors in the county to whom they are relating. Statistics show that they have cut in half the number of pastoral changes within the county. They have a wide-ranging program of continuing education, including courses on how to edit the church newsletter (taught by a local newspaper editor), alcoholic counseling (directed by the local hospital), research projects on rural America (done in conjunction with a seminary in Chicago, whose faculty make trips to the county). They have a credit union holding over two hundred thousand dollars in assets, which made thirteen loans during the year. They purchased eight Chevrolet automobiles from a local dealer at volume purchase price. They had continuing dialogues with churches and judicatories about pastoral vacancies in the area. They have recently developed church profiles to help prospective pastors understand a particular church, and of course they have interpretive materials about the association, which they give to new pastors upon their arrival. They had a grand three-day excursion to Chicago, a golf league in the summer, and a bowling league in the winter. They also have a committee working on the feasibility of building a retirement complex for clergy within Galilee County.

What is more, there is a new spirit within the churches of the county. The congregations feel much better about themselves and their ministers. Even denominational executives make it a point to visit the plenary sessions and chat with participants. The seminary has never done more teaching than it is now doing in the county. And when the local newspaper writes about the professional association the readers know what it is and take an interest.

Isn't it fun to hypothesize? You can make anything happen—which is exactly the point. You can do it too. Good organizations are born from ambitious dreams.

Now let me present, not a dream, but a reality. By comparison it may sound small and unproductive, but in fact it is the pilot professional association. It does exist and is functioning, and that's the important point.

A Workshop on Professional Associations

Report from the Field

In January 1974, twenty clergymen of the Illinois Conference of the United Church of Christ met for a denominationally-sponsored program called "Crossroads." On a cold winter morning I came to that group, along with several others, as a resource leader. I introduced this presentation, as I had to many other groups. It was a pop in, pop off, and pop out performance. I don't like that format, but it is common in many such gatherings.

I was mildly surprised a few weeks later when I was invited to meet with a small group of clergy. It seems that after I left, twelve of the participators at Crossroads had written and signed a covenant to create a professional association. Now the group was meeting to draw up a proposed constitution and by-laws. They wanted to clarify a couple of matters I had raised. I did meet with them—and I smiled a lot.

About six months later I received a mimeographed letter inviting me to the first organizing meeting of the Professional Association of Clergy (PAC) in Illinois. The constitution and by-laws were enclosed. An application card for membership was added, fee thirty dollars. I sent them the card and the money, but did not attend the meeting.

A year later I went to the annual judicatory meeting, and there at a booth in the exhibit area, passing out buttons and brochures and enlisting members, was the Professional Association of Clergy. They greeted me in a jovial mood, calling me the "godfather." The meeting agenda included a presentation by the association which resulted in several resolutions. Included was a call for the development of a local church profile for prospective pastors, and a pledge of a nondiscriminatory policy toward women ministers and pastors over the age of fifty–five. These passed (although in free church polity this was not necessarily a change of practice). I was so proud that day.

And the story goes on. I have participated as a member of the Professional Association of Clergy in Illinois, but never in a leadership capacity. That they have without me. Let me quote the membership director's report verbatim: "As of January 1, 1978, the active membership of PAC is 101. Nine of these are new members. Twenty-two who were members in 1976 opted out. In addition, many are affiliate members by virtue of their membership in the credit union. One person withdrew his membership in midyear because he felt PAC was not meeting his needs."

Sorry about that one, but what a terrific report! The reference to affiliate members concerns a group of Christian ministers (Disciples of Christ) who want to participate in the credit union, but not in PAC. At the time the credit union had $187,000 in assets; it had made twenty-three loans in the last year, none had defaulted, paid a dividend of 5¼ percent, and proposed that the membership offer certificates of deposit at higher interest rates. The credit union report, without naming names, listed some of the special circumstances restricting loans.

PAC has had many continuing education offerings, from preaching workshops to courses in personal financial management. They offer subscriptions to professional magazines for the membership. They had an all-day fun day for member families at a nearby resort.

In all candor, some attempts failed. The fleet purchasing of cars has not worked out, although they are still trying—it seems there is too much variety in automotive needs to make a volume purchase. Nothing has been done about orienting the beginner or relating to retired clergy, and I have no data on salaries or placement changes. But they are all on the PAC agenda.

The point of this report from the field is that some clergy have taken the agenda seriously. They have moved within a denominational context to be responsible for themselves. They, and I, are proud of what they have done. The fact that PAC has been in existence five years does not alone make it a success, but when you compare it to what was being done before, it is a whopping accomplishment.

Adjournment and Benediction

The last item on an agenda at church gatherings is adjournment and benediction. At such gatherings, before the last vote is taken and the final amen is said, participants inevitably begin to review what has happened in their minds. What have we done here? What is of temporary and what is of lasting value? What must I do now in response to this gathering? These concluding words are written to facilitate that review and assimilation process.

The keynote section put forth an analysis of forces affecting the parish clergy. It was stated that parish clergy find themselves affected by the seminary, the laity, the denominational church, and the culture. If greater reciprocity between these forces and the clergy themselves seems desirable, then the ministerial profession must exercise greater responsibility for its own direction, conduct, and values. This analysis was followed by seven specific resolutions advocating the goals we could pursue if we were to assume responsibility for our profession. Finally, some notes were penned on the style and shape of a professional association that would seek to pursue such common goals. Throughout the keynote, advocacy, and organizational development sections, a basic insight was utilized. The parish clergy have a vertical career pattern, i.e., they enter the practice of ministry and perform its functions throughout a lifetime. However, the church systems, which affect the clergy, are based on horizontal relationships. In these systems the minister's role is confined almost exclusively to relating to his or her congregation. The most important idea in this whole book is the call for more attention to and intention about the vertical dimension within the church systems. This call, coupled with an affirmation about our collective power, forms the challenge of this book.

As you weigh in your mind and heart what personal and collective response you can make to this analysis and this challenge, you may welcome some commentary on integrating this agenda or these professional concerns, within the larger ministerial *milieu.*

The Context of Ministry

The parish church is not an island, isolated and remote from the terrain of a particular time and place. In our time and place children are bitten by rats in the squalor of their homes; grown men and women have the distended bellies of world starvation; the jails hold prisoners of the earth condemned for their ideas, their protests against injustice, their faith. In such a brutal and brutalizing world, to advocate defining success for oneself seems not only irrelevant and irresponsible, but downright irreligious and irrational. The pain of our world, in its manifold dimensions and places, may be a better agenda for parish clergy.

In this world, at this time and place, there is poverty of spirit. In the dripping affluence of suburbia there are cries in the night of lives founded upon shifting sands. In the temples of commerce wicked ways enslave and hold captive prisoners of crass and inhumane values and ethics. Amidst hamlets and urban sprawl the psychic pain of interpersonal relationships is a constant, intruding presence. This world hurts for the lack of words and deeds of faith, the power of spiritual strength, the wisdom of morality, and the simple decency of those who give first priority to the Spirit. In such a deprived world, to advocate higher salaries seems not only irrelevant and irresponsible, but irreligious and irrational as well.

The great Christian church, in all cultures, and in all its divisions, spreads before us in pain and need. Sadly divided by the tenacity of historic movements, sadly stripped of its potency and primacy by a world hellbent on secularization, engaged in a life and death battle with the many "isms" of this world that vie for control of heart and mind, this embattled church is still God's possessive agency for mission in the world. In an institution so beleaguered, to advocate peer participation in placement seems irrelevant and irresponsible, not to mention irreligious and irrational.

133

The sickness of this time and place is virulent in your own local church. While you spend time reading these words, within a local church somewhere—maybe your own parish—someone else suffers an addiction, a loss, a shocking betrayal which goes unnoticed, unrequited, uncared for. When local churches are such frail reeds, to advocate greater selectivity for older ministers seems irrelevant and irresponsible and irreligious and irrational.

Are the clergy being urged to tune their violins while Rome and its environs burn? Have you been challenged to a new narcissism relevant only to Tom Wolfe's "Let's Talk About Me" world? I disavow these conclusions, so how shall I respond to these questions?

One of the unheralded talents of parish clergy is a rare and unusual ability to function simultaneously at many levels of being. When a preacher speaks from the pulpit, the words are uttered not only for the handful in the pews, but also for those who are not there, those who cannot speak the language, those who cannot hear these particular words. Genuine preaching spreads in concentric circles and woe to the preacher who shrinks the scope of the Gospel!

So it is with this professional agenda; it is not the only challenge before the parish clergy. This agenda is one of many, and will take its place amidst and among others. You will take hold of it wherever it belongs in your scheme of things. My rationale for writing is that you begin where you are with this agenda and move outward in ever-enlarging circles. There is no immediate connection between this agenda and the cataclysms of the world and the church in these times, except as it may change for the better the small portion of the world which overlaps *with* your particular time and place. A chain of effect can be broken and severed at any point, but the links are these: a revitalized clergy affecting the church, a revitalized church affecting the culture, and a revitalized culture affecting the world's communities, but the beginning link is a revitalized clergy affecting their immediate colleagues.

This book has a narrow focus: the parish clergy. But its challenge is the stewardship of that special group. It is sad to see the energy of such a group unrealized. It is a joy to conceive of ways in which that energy can be released for other, more worthwhile, pursuits. Although the advocacies are stated with an apparent clerical chauvinism, if this area of concern is left unaddressed the issues of the clergy will usurp the available energy of the profession. But if enacted, these advocacies could save the profession from waste. It is a function of stewardship to stop waste and redirect energy into more productive uses.

At this point of adjournment, muse for yourself and with your colleagues on the stewardship of your profession, its wastes and its potentials. Such musings will guide you in inserting this agenda among the many of our time and place.

The Gripe Syndrome

As you review the analyses and advocacies of this book, you may feel they are trivial. Examined negatively these seven advocacies are not much more than articulated gripes that clergy have about their work. I told you in the introduction that this book was neither a theological fish nor a sociological fowl, but one pastor's pastoral experi-

135

ence. I could have said then, but did not, that this agenda was formed by listening to clergy talk about their practice. My seven advocacies are each rooted in a recurrent slice of life that colleagues have whispered or roared into my ears. I did say that personally I had never felt victimized at any one of these points, and I have not. But my experience with each of these areas has made me tender and attentive, sensitive toward an understanding of what clergy mean and how they feel when they complain about their profession.

Gripe is not one of my favorite words because it is pejorative—it connotes inconsequential complaint about nonessential matters. If we call a gripe a pain or an ache, we elevate the same complaint to one of greater consequence. If you listen to preacher-talk you will hear griping about first parishes, their continuing education experiences, their salaries, their placement, their burdens at work, and their retirement, and all of this will be clothed in confusion about success. I refuse to believe that all such talk can be dismissed as mere griping.

Any lament about things as they are experienced—whether you call it a gripe or an ache—is also a plea, a plea that implies a hope for alteration. The difference between a gripe and a plea is not what one says, but what one does about that experience. If one does not wish to change, whether oneself or one's condition, then one is a griper, probably chronically and perpetually. But when the opportunity comes for change, to alter the experience of things as they are, and one seizes that opportunity, then one's gripe becomes a plea.

I think *The New Shape of Ministry* can be a response to our pleas, but ultimately that is not for me to judge. Nor is it for you, individually, to judge. It is for us to judge, collectively, as colleagues in the practice of a profession. This book could be a turning point. Your response to its advocacies will divide the gripers from those who really plea for alteration. If there is nothing acceptable in these visions of reform then the profession can continue to gripe over the tender points of friction. But when we hear that grumbling, we will know what it means.

If the crunch points noted here are only annoyances then surely we can live with them and gripe about them at will. But if they do have substance and change seems appropriate, then more work on these matters lies before us. Your discerning review of the issues you think appropriate for this agenda is a start, but there is more, much more, yet to be done.

Research and Development

In a sense, this book is a luxury. In another sense it is a model. It is a luxury because it is gratuitous, meaning it was neither commissioned nor requested. It is not the result of a long and costly study. It is a model because it was written by a practitioner of the profession, whereas most books about ministry are written by others. Perhaps this is one of the reasons clergy tend to think the matters which touch their lives most directly (matters about which they already have data and conjectures concerning consequences) are of little relevance to them personally.

This model has a similar purpose to what is known in business as research and development. Companies that are successful in the manufacture and sale of certain products are precisely those that reinvest a portion of their earnings to discover better ways of serving their customers or develop new products for new potential markets. What I find commendable is the idea that a portion of the returns gleaned in doing a particular task is plowed back into more research and development regarding that service. At its best, this book is just that: research and development about the ministerial profession. For me, personally, its preparation was a tithe of my professional experience—a way of giving back to my colleagues a report and interpretation of my data gathered from eighteen years of professional practice—with the intent of developing the whole profession.

This is the model offered to you. As a parish pastor you may have dismissed every bit of my interpretation and strategy, but if so you still have a model for reflecting on what you know about the practice of ministry and a means for sharing this with your colleagues. Sharing of information and interpretation is scant in the profession, and in the absence of our own networks of communication we let others be the primary spokespersons to us and for us. Your own research and development may be as simple as musing about what affects the parish clergy; it may be as complex as an attempt to organize a professional association. In such ways you too can offer a tithe to your profession.

Problems and Possibilities

The focus of this book, looking for and examining what can be changed, has of necessity directed your attention to problem areas within the profession. A word of balance needs to be offered in this adjourning statement.

I hope that I have rightly named the central professional

problems and brought them to your attention through this agenda. The deficiency of my approach is the implication that the profession is a morass of problems, that their cumulative effect represents a horrendous nightmare of inadequacies and poses a terrible burden. I don't believe that for an instant, and this word of balance may help to correct the excessively negative and critical slant of this book.

The greatest asset of our profession is the concomitant presence of freedom and commitment. No other vocation offers its practitioners so much personal freedom. Many a parish minister has taken a hobby or special interest and baptized it a ministry. By and large, parish clergy get to do what they like to do. Jim Glasse has spoken to us of "paying the rent," meaning that there are certain expectations of performance that have to be met. But they are relatively few, and the majority of our work is what we want it to be. It is the presence of commitment that keeps our personal freedom from degenerating into license. Most parish clergy want to use their talents, no matter what their form, in the service of Christ and the church.

Another real asset of the profession is its people-centered stance. It used to bother me when my children would ask me, "What did you do today?" My recitation of the events of my day inevitably consisted of a list of conversations—I had spent my day talking to people. Somehow this seemed trivial and mundane. But the larger truth is that those people may have ranged in age from seven to seventy; they may have been sad or glad; they may have been friends with whom I regularly associated, or strangers I would never see again. But my day, my years, were filled with people in their infinite variety. What keeps the minister from being just a social butterfly, again, is commitment. We are helpers and enablers of all such people who fill our days.

Because we come to expect it in others, parish clergy sometimes underestimate the opportunities that they have to grow in faith. Lay people simply do not have the constant stimuli that we have to our faith. Even a paying the rent task like the weekly sermon requires us to think about the faith. I have had my share of plateaus and dry spells, but the disciplines of my profession in study and prayer have carried me forward in a pilgrimage of faith. I have not finished the course, but I have grown enormously in my personal faith. And the faith I have and the way it has grown has been through disciplined commitment. And it is shared all the time in so many ways with the people I encounter.

Finally, parish clergy are caretakers of some precious symbols. Many of the significant moments in my ministry have not been moments in which my personal skill effected an important change in the life of another. The change had been lurking in the person's soul all the time, it just needed liberation. The Episcopal Church has preserved the title of vicar to refer to its parish clergy. If you look up that word in a dictionary you will find that "representative figure" is one of its meanings. Often it is not I, but that representative symbol that effects change in people's lives. Centuries ago in its struggles to know its rightful mind in the midst of heretical views, the Christian church affirmed that the efficacy of the sacrament was not dependent upon the character of the officiant. This is still true, and as custodians of the symbols of the priestly office we still so function. That is our true power: not in who we are, but in what we represent.

Symbols are the treasures of the ministerial profession. We do have our problems, and we must address them and cope with them as we can. But as long as we share the faith with others in freedom and commitment, practice the disciplines, and keep the perspective of our representative role, no problem or sets of problems will deter us from the pilgrimage upon which we are engaged.

Finally, Brethren

The final admonition of this book is a return to our original contract, which was to keep in mind that the specific formulations of this book are not essential to its purpose. Whatever confirmations you can make from your own pastoral experience are welcomed. Whatever alternatives you think preferable are equally welcomed. These are important concerns of the entire ministerial profession. I do not have unconditional faith about the way I have presented these issues, nor necessarily in the solutions proposed. I do have unconditional faith that if we will collectively direct our mighty energies and resources to the agenda of the parish clergy, the accurate and relevant interpretations and resolutions will emerge.

The title of this work contains an important proposition. It is called *The New Shape of Ministry.* The title was conceived in hope, the hope that we will own for ourselves this agenda, that in our many denominational forms, faiths, and personal variables, we, parish clergy, will accept responsibility for our profession. The writing is done, let the responses begin.

Benediction

> God be with you. May the
> Spirit of God in Christ go
> where you go; guide where
> you must make choices;
> comfort where you hurt;
> and surprise you by the constancy
> of Love for what you are
> and what you do.